A SPIRITUAL HOUSE

A SPIRITUAL HOUSE

Reflections on some current ethical issues

by W. Pouwelse

PREMIER PUBLISHING
WINNIPEG

Pouwelse, W., 1928—
A spiritual house

ISBN 0-88756-032-6
1. Christian ethics — Reformed authors.
2. Christian life — Reformed authors. I. Title.
BJ1251.P673 1986   241'.045732   C86-098079-0

FIRST PRINTING — MAY 1986
SECOND PRINTING — APRIL 1988
THIRD PRINTING — OCTOBER 1991

PREMIER PUBLISHING
ONE BEGHIN AVENUE, WINNIPEG, MANITOBA, CANADA R2J 3X5

PREFACE

This book is a follow-up or continuation of my previously published *LIKE LIVING STONES*. In the first volume I discussed a number of issues concerning family life. Special attention was paid to marriage, bringing forth children, the value of human life, and some aspects of life and death.

In this book I will focus more specifically on the raising and educating of children, and the position of special groups in our society. Attention will be paid to the social aspects of society, the relationship between employer and employee, and the influence of the news media in this respect. The last chapter deals with the importance of prayer.

Because the title of this book has been taken from the same chapter of the Bible, I will repeat what I wrote in the preface of my previous book. In I Peter 2 the apostle admonishes his audience to live in such a way that the name of God may be glorified. He calls Jesus Christ the cornerstone of the *spiritual house*, the ground and rock of our salvation. Thankful for this precious gift, we have to offer our whole life as a spiritual sacrifice, acceptable to God through Jesus Christ. Doing so, we will become *like living stones* in *a spiritual house*, of which Jesus Christ is the cornerstone.

As we aim to live to the glory of God, we have to face and to clear up many practical questions. Many issues in everyday life call for an answer. Ethical decisions have to be made. Not in every situation is it clear cut which route we have to go. Many aspects have to be considered.

In this book I will try to help you in coming to grips with some current issues. On most of the topics I have published a series of articles in the Canadian Reformed magazine *Clarion*. In response to the reactions received, I decided to rework some of the material for publication as a book. The setup of this book allows it to be used as reading material, but also as an outline for discussion in the study societies. I hope that it may serve as a guideline for many discussions and that it may give some food for thought in a turbulent world.

That we ourselves, *like living stones*, may be built into *A SPIRITUAL HOUSE* (cf. I Peter 2:5), to be a holy priesthood, to offer spiritual sacrifices acceptable to God through Jesus Christ, is the sincere desire of

THE AUTHOR

Langley, B.C.   December 1985

CONTENTS

CHAPTER IV

The position of handicapped children

CHAPTER V

The position of elderly people

CHAPTER VI

The task of a mother in a family

CHAPTER VII

The relationship between employer and employee

CHAPTER VIII

Organized labour

CHAPTER IX

Our position on lotteries

CHAPTER X

The influence of the news media

CHAPTER XI

The importance of prayer

INTRODUCTION

In most chapters of this book ethical issues are discussed. Ethics is the science which deals with morals. Questions about right and wrong have to be answered. That is not always an easy task. Most questions to be dealt with in Christian ethics arise from new situations or developments, for which no rules or moral standards have been formulated yet. If there is a clear rule or commandment in Holy Scripture, we need not discuss the matter. The Word of God decides. However, in most cases there is not such a clear commandment. In such practical situations we have to find our way, using our own responsibility and listening to each other, being on the alert to resist all temptations to give in to wrong or dangerous developments.

An important aspect of Christian ethics is that we have to be consistent and not opportunistic. Therefore we often have to judge by analogy, going by what is a "generally accepted" practice. Such a reasoning does not make a generally accepted matter a moral standard, but it gives us an important help. It works and has value in two directions. If a judgment by analogy seems to justify something, while at the same time we feel, for one reason or another, that it is not quite right, then we are confronted with an inconsistency. We will have to reconsider whether the previously "generally accepted" matter was and still is right. It might very well be, and it has happened more often, that such a reasoning drives us to the conclusion that we have derailed somewhere along the line and are on the wrong track, without being aware of it. Therefore we consider it important in Christian ethics to judge by analogy. There is a rapid development in every area of human life, and we often have to make a decision on the spur of the moment. We cannot always consider or fathom the consequences of a decision. A custom may develop, and we may consider something a generally accepted practice, without realizing what the consequences are in the long run. However, "generally accepted" matters might appear not to be as innocent as they seemed at the first glance. Things are sometimes much more complicated and penetrate our life in a more subtle way than we are aware of. Therefore ongoing study and discussion is necessary. Reasoning by analogy can be of great help in this respect.

That is why I will try, in what follows, to make a contribution in this ongoing discussion, to find our way in everyday life, in accordance with the Word of God.

Childrearing and discipline

1. An outdated system?

In this first chapter I will deal with some aspects of childrearing and discipline. It is important to listen first to what the Bible says in this respect. Therefore we will pay attention to a number of texts, in which this issue is mentioned.

The most important fact is that discipline is a matter of love. That applies to every relationship in which we are confronted with authority and the obligation to obey. The discipline exercised by the civil government is different from the discipline exercised by the office-bearers in the church, and parents will discipline their children in a different way than the teachers at school. However, the basic rule and guideline for every form of discipline has to be love, the intention to help, to correct, to educate, or even to rehabilitate the subject.

Proverbs 13:24 says that to "spare the rod" means to "hate" your son, while love makes one diligent to discipline. In Hebrews 12:6 the Bible teaches us that the Lord shows His love in the way He disciplines us, while those who do not receive discipline are considered "illegitimate children." Discipline, even corporal punishment, has to be based upon and carried out in love.

Today this is considered to be outdated. According to the principles of modern pedagogy, children should be left free. No moral standards and values should be imposed on them; they should be given the opportunity to develop their own standards and their own value system. Their individual development is disturbed when adults, either parents or teachers, instill in them certain ideas. They should be provided only with factual information, and even that should be subject to their own preferences. They should not be bothered too much by what the teacher thinks is important; they should be occupied with what personally interests them. In this way they can freely develop their own personality and their own ideas about good and evil. They can freely grow according to their intrinsic capacities.

That is the concept of modern, humanistic childrearing and education. In this philosophy there is no place for discipline, let alone corporal punishment. No parent or teacher has the right to impose his ideas on such a tender child; he is too vulnerable to be treated so roughly. It would do lasting and irreparable damage to his concept of justice and create feelings of frustration, aversion and rebellion in the mind of the child.

This whole theory is based on a humanistic idea about mankind.

Mankind is good in itself. Evil thoughts and actions result from environmental influences. A human being, left to himself, without any bad influence, is supposed to develop into a perfect being; at least he has the potential to do so, according to this theory.

This idea has been preached and practised in education everywhere. Some have followed it only to a certain extent, others have gone all the way, to the very extreme. However, it does not work. The generation of children educated according to these principles, is not happier, more satisfied and more mature and independent, with a greater awareness of responsibility than the previous generation. On the contrary. There is disappointment, disillusionment, emptiness and sometimes even desperation. According to statistics, the suicide rate among teenagers in the U.S.A. has climbed to an all-time high of five thousand a year, while for each of these registered cases there are about fifty to a hundred youngsters who unsuccessfully attempt to commit suicide. Besides this, according to specialists, many fatal teenage accidents are disguised suicides. This is an alarming development instead of an encouraging result of modern childrearing and education methods and practices.

2. Anarchy

The results of the modern approach not only are evident in the private lives of teenagers, as the statistics about suicide show, but also are felt in public life, in the schools and in the families.

It is a well-known fact that there is a growing uneasiness among the teachers in public schools. Some have given up their jobs because they cannot handle the problems any longer. Others feel threatened in the classroom and are afraid to use disciplinary measure or to reprimand a student, because they might be physically attacked by the students. Some have taken courses in self-defence. In some schools there is little enforcement of the rules and anarchy creeps in.

The same happens in public life. The police force is unable to enforce the law. If they act against juvenile crime, they often have to face much criticism, resistance and red tape. At the same time mass demonstrations against legislation enacted by a democratically elected government can force the government to back down, to give in, to change the law or to abstain from enforcing a current law. Not what the law says is right, but what public opinion propagates. And this so-called public opinion is often the voice of the most vocal and aggressive action group or the group which manages to attract the most coverage by the news media.

The humanistic approach proclaims freedom for everyone. The slogan of the French revolution is still alive: fraternity, liberty and equality. However, the result is a loss of freedom and the imposition of the rules of the strongest pressure group upon the silent majority. It is the law of the jungle, bringing about lawlessness, chaos, violence, and a spirit of revolution. The final result is anarchy.

Today we hear about hijackings, kidnappings, rapes, murders, break-ins and other acts of violence as never before. It is no longer safe to walk

on the street in the evening and in some areas women and children are not even safe on the street in clear daylight, if they are without protection. In many of these crimes, teenagers are involved. According to statistics more seventeen to twenty-year-old males are involved in almost every class of crime, including homicide, than in any other age group. The new approach in childrearing did not make the new generation happier. Instead, it made them desperate. The decline in moral standards is not caused by the bad economic situation, or the high unemployment rate. It is not poverty that brings about anarchy, but affluence and (first and foremost) the lack of loving discipline.

3. Biblical guidelines

In this chapter I will discuss some aspects of discipline. I will first pay attention to the Biblical task of those who are in a position of authority and those who are subject to it. This authority begins in the home. That is where children are first confronted with authority and loving discipline. That is where they have to learn the basic rules of authority and discipline. If they are not taught to obey authority and to appreciate loving discipline as something that protects and guides their life, they will never rightly understand the meaning and value of it.

Lord's Day 39 of the Heidelberg Catechism says that I have to "show all honour, love, and faithfulness to my father and mother and to all those in authority over me, . . . since it is God's will to govern us by their hand." Discipline may be unpleasant at the moment, but children should be taught and should experience that it is a relationship of loving care. In Hebrews 12:11 we read: "For the moment all discipline seems painful rather than pleasant; later it yields the peaceful fruit of righteousness to those who have been trained by it."

The two texts, "He who spares the rod hates his son, but he who loves him is diligent to discipline him" (Proverbs 13:24) and "The Lord disciplines him whom he loves" (Hebrews 12:6) contain the ongoing teaching of Holy Scripture. Discipline is not a matter of being tough and merciless. On the contrary. Discipline is and should always be a matter of tender loving care. It is to protect the subject against a danger of which he may not even be aware. It is to keep the child on the right track and to teach him what really matters in life. In Proverbs 1:7 we read: "The fear of the LORD is the beginning of knowledge; fools despise wisdom and understanding." That is the basic rule and foundation of all instruction and discipline. The word *fear* in this text does not first of all mean anxiety, being afraid of some punishment that might be coming, but it means to have a great respect and regard for the LORD and His commandments, to obey Him in thankful submission.

In allowing children to be free and by letting them grow up without discipline, we are not doing them a favour. Proverbs 13:24 says instead that it is a matter of hate. It means denying the children one of the most elementary "rights." The Lord Himself shows His love towards us in the

15

way He disciplines us. Those who do not receive discipline are called "illegitimate children."

Parents should not be afraid that corporal punishment, used with love, will damage their children. Proverbs 23:13,14 says: "Do not withhold discipline from a child; if you beat him with a rod he will not die. If you beat him with a rod you will save his life from Sheol." That is clear language. He will not die; on the contrary, he will live; he will be saved from Sheol. Proverbs 22:15 says: "Folly is bound up in the heart of a child, but the rod of discipline drives it far from him."

Also Proverbs 29:15 speaks about the instruction received via loving discipline. "The rod of reproof gives wisdom, but a child left to himself brings shame to his mother." That is what we very often see. Children who are left to themselves and do not get the discipline they ought to receive, finally bring shame to their parents. That is the result of a lack of loving discipline. That is what Proverbs 13:24 calls "hating" your child.

This discipline should not begin when a child becomes a teenager, because then it is too late and the damage is done. It should start right from the beginning. Proverbs 19:18 says: "Discipline your son while there is still hope; do not set your heart on his destruction." The absence of discipline, at an early age, is called "his destruction."

Such discipline is not always felt as an act of love, not even when parents are well aware of the purpose of discipline and exercise it in a fair and consistent manner, with tender loving care. In Hebrews 12:11 we read: "For the moment all discipline seems painful rather than pleasant; later it yields the peaceful fruit of righteousness to those who have been trained by it." When we stick to the Biblical rules of loving discipline, the children will sooner or later acknowledge that the parents have shown them tender loving care in exercising discipline. They will "yield the peaceful fruits of righteousness," instead of the bitter fruits of unrighteousness, lawlessness and desperation, caused by a lack of discipline.

Now that we have discussed the Biblical rules, principles and guidelines for discipline, we will turn our attention to a number of practical aspects of discipline.

4. Growing to maturity

The statements that children do not like to be disciplined, that they should not be disciplined, and that they prefer freedom (no rules), are simply not true. In the previous section we have seen that the Bible clearly teaches us: "He who spares the rod hates his son, but he who loves him is diligent to discipline him." Experience shows that we cannot ignore this divine rule without doing great harm to children and to society at large. It might be true that children, for a short time, enjoy the absence of authority and enforcement of rules. They like to get off track once in a while. But in the long run they get a feeling of security when there is fair and consistent discipline. They know that they do not always do the right thing and that they sometimes cannot gauge the consequences of their deeds. It gives them a sense of security to know that somehow, somewhere, someone is taking care of them; someone is keeping them from going too far off track; someone is ready to help if they really get into trouble. It gives them a feeling of security to know that, if worse comes to worst, someone will step in and help them.

Many examples can be mentioned. If a teacher cannot maintain order in the classroom, the children enjoy it for a while, but they finally get tired of it and do not appreciate it at all. They feel that no one is at the helm and that their time is being wasted. They become bored and the situation runs out of control. On the other hand, if a teacher maintains order in a strict, fair and consistent manner, the children may at first say that they do not like it very much and that the teacher is "strict," but in the long run they love the teacher; they respect him and enjoy his discipline.

The same counts for parents. It is not true that children are better off and happier when the parents do not impose certain guidelines and definite rules. On the contrary. They are dissatisfied and bored and finally become rebellious. Because they have never learned to obey rules, they will not even be able to cooperate and work together with others according to certain rules. They have missed a very important thing in their life, and that is learning self-restraint and respect for others.

A young and tender plant cannot grow to maturity without being guided in the right direction. Neither can a child develop to maturity in a proper way without the guidance and direction of loving discipline. Guidance in growing to maturity is no less necessary than food. The greatest source of unhappiness among teenagers is that they have been denied one of the most elementary things in growing to maturity: loving discipline.

As I mentioned earlier, such discipline should be fair and consistent. These are the next points on which we will focus our attention.

5. Discipline should be fair

Every form of authority and discipline should be fair. That applies to parents, to teachers, to the civil government in its law-enforcement and in its judicial system, and to the discipline exercised by the church.

Children, in general and in the long run, do not mind strict discipline, as long as it is fair. They have a strong feeling for fairness. If children feel that the punishment or the disciplinary measure is not fair, the authority, be it parent, teacher, or whoever, should try to explain the reason behind it, but parents or teachers should not open a debate about the correctness of their decision. Many decisions will not be appreciated or agreed upon at the time the discipline is exercised. Children always like a little more room to maneuver, and they want to see how far they can go. The final decision should be up to the one in authority.

However, wanting a little more freedom or disagreeing with a decision is something quite different from feeling that it is unfair. If children are punished for some wrongdoing, they do not immediately appreciate the punishment. In Hebrews 12:11 we read: "For the moment all discipline seems painful rather than pleasant; later it yields the peaceful fruit of righteousness to those who have been trained by it." However, if children

17

are wrongfully accused of something or are punished for what they have not done, they will feel it is unfair. It may also happen that they are punished much more severely than they had expected. The reason can be that they do not understand the impact or the seriousness of their wrongdoing. It is also possible that the parent or the teacher just happens to be in a bad mood on account of completely unrelated matters and that the children receive the recompense for the unvented frustration of the one in authority. In both cases the children will feel that they are being treated unfairly, and rightly so.

In the first situation the parent or teacher should try to explain to the children why they are being treated and punished so severely. It should be made clear to them that what they have done is for one reason or another exceptionally serious. That makes the discipline much more effective and avoids unnecessary feelings of unfairness.

It is also possible that the punishment was too severe, or even unjustified, because the parent or the teacher made a wrong presumption about guiltiness or a wrong assessment of the situation. It is even possible that the authority later feels that his decision was made in a fit of anger. In such a situation the authority should not hesitate to correct the measure as best as possible, and to admit that he made an error in his judgment.

Some parents are afraid that their authority will be undermined if they admit that they have been wrong. The opposite is true. Children do not lose respect for a parent or teacher who admits that he has made a mistake. They only learn that also those in authority are mere human beings who make mistakes. They will appreciate the fact that they are fair after all, and that they have the courage to admit their mistakes. The result is that the parent or teacher remains at the helm and is respected by the child even more.

This is a completely different situation than when a child tries to challenge the authority. That children try out authority or even challenge it is part of the game. If that is the case, they should be answered in a proper way, and no child will be shocked to find out the hard way that he may not challenge authority. To try out authority is also a matter of seeing how "real" it is. If children find out that they can challenge the authority and that the parent or the teacher gives in and does not "stand the test," they may seem to enjoy it for a while and see it as a victory, but basically they are disappointed. Their trust and confidence is gone. They do not feel secure any longer.

One of the most important aspects of authority and discipline is that children feel that they are protected against going too far off track, and that parents will use their moral authority to help them out when they really get into trouble. However, if the person in authority cannot stand the "test" of being challenged by children, the children will not have much confidence in him when it really comes to the point that they need help.

6. Discipline should be consistent

Another important aspect of discipline is consistency. Also in this respect children are very sensitive. Inconsistency makes them feel insecure. They do not know what to expect and what to obey. If parents sometimes close their eyes when their children clearly violate the rules or ignore authority and at other times severely punish them for the same thing, the children lose their feeling of justice. They do not know what to expect and feel that they are at the mercy of the authority. That is devastating for their development. They have to learn what it means to obey the rules and what the consequences of ignoring the rules are. They will readily learn their lesson if they know what is coming and what they can expect. It is confusing always to be in limbo about what is going to happen. It will not give them the correct view of what justice is all about.

Once, years ago, I heard a story which struck me and showed me the importance of consistency in discipline. A widow, whose youngest child was about four years old, tried to teach the boy good behaviour. Once he had done something he knew was wrong and would result in a spanking. However, his mother was so concerned and occupied with other things that she paid little attention to what the boy had done. She cleaned up the mess he had made and left it at that without any disciplinary measure. The result was that the boy became confused. He expected punishment, but it did not come, and he did not understand why. He even drew a completely wrong conclusion. After a while he approached his mother and said, "Do you not love me any longer?" His mother was surprised and asked, "Why do you say that?" His reaction stunned the mother. He said, "I deserved a spanking, but you did not care about me." This reaction, strange as it may seem, clearly shows that an inconsistency in discipline made the boy feel insecure. He did not mind getting spanked when he deserved it, but he got upset and confused when his mother failed to exercise loving discipline in a consistent manner.

7. Teaching a value system

One of the main goals in teaching a value system is to eliminate or discourage bad behaviour and to teach good behaviour in an effective way.

To be able to make decisions in their own lives, children need a value system to relate to. Such a value system has to be developed and learned. That can only be done by proper guidance. It is wrong and very dangerous to leave it up to the teenager to develop this on his own. It not only makes him feel insecure, as we have seen before, but it also denies him the guidance he needs and deserves. It puts him in great danger. He may develop a completely wrong value system because of his lack of experience. He has to learn everything the hard way. It also conflicts with the Word of God. Parents and teachers have the duty to teach the children the one and only correct value system according to the Word of God. In Proverbs 29:15 we read: "A child left to himself brings shame to his mother."

There are basically two ways to teach a value system: by discouraging bad behaviour and by encouraging good behaviour. Both principles have to be applied simultaneously and in a balanced manner, because the one does not work without the other.

Discipline and punishment are meant to discourage bad behaviour. One of the basic principles is that children, as well as adults, do many things not just for the fun of it, but for the pleasant, desired results or consequences of the actions. Although (fortunately) many people enjoy their daily job, many would do their work with considerably less enthusiasm if they did not have the prospect of a pay cheque at the end of the week or the month.

Money is not the only reward. Making other people happy or being respected by others can also give satisfaction and can encourage people to do a job which they otherwise would not appreciate very much.

Another reason for doing or not doing something can be the awareness that punishment will follow. Obeying traffic rules or paying tax may not be our favourite activities, but the enforcement of the law by the civil government makes us prefer to obey rather than to get a ticket or to pay a fine. That is also a matter of considering the consequences, in this case the consequence of not being bothered by penalties. Of course, for a Christian the main reason for obedience should be that the Lord requires from us that we respect the authorities. We should not obey the Lord out of fear of punishment, but in thankfulness for all that He has given to us in Jesus Christ our Lord.

And yet, satisfaction and reward are important factors in human behaviour. Psalm 19:11 says that in keeping the ordinances of the LORD there is great reward, and in Proverbs 11:18 we read: "A wicked man earns deceptive wages, but one who sows righteousness gets a sure reward." As is the case with many things, we should not make it an either-or issue, but we have to be aware of the fact that it is the one as well as the other. The same counts for children. They have to obey their parents in love. Lord's Day 39 of the Heidelberg Catechism says that I have to show honour, love, and faithfulness to my father and mother. Still we have to use positive encouragement and reinforcement in education no less than discipline and retribution to discourage bad behaviour.

8. Discouraging bad behaviour

The process of discouraging undesirable behaviour begins very early in a child's life, before he himself is even aware of it. When a toddler does something without having the slightest idea about right or wrong, but he finds out that it always has unpleasant consequences, he will give up. On the other hand he will be encouraged to do something if he feels that it has pleasant results. This happens without his being aware of it. It is just a natural reaction. A baby usually cries when he feels uncomfortable. But if the baby is held and cuddled every time he cries, he will associate the rather unpleasant activity of crying with some pleasant results and simply "communicate" in this way. He will cry more often, because he likes to be cuddled. This simple principle counts for almost every situation.

Discipline has to be used as a punishment, to show and let the children feel that they have to obey authority. That is certainly an important aspect of it. However, no less important is the sometimes subtle effect of discouraging wrong behaviour. Bad behaviour, no matter whether it is a wrong habit, an intended challenging of the authority, or an attempt to get away with something the children know is wrong, should never be rewarded. If they feel that it is not worth trying and that the result is worse than the pleasure derived from it, they will give up and comply with the rules.

9. Encouraging good behaviour

We have seen in the previous section that discipline plays an important role in discouraging bad behaviour. The encouragement of good behaviour plays an equally important role in the teaching of a value system.

Let me use a simple example to explain. Some parents are very concerned because their children come home late and go out too often. They set a certain time for coming home and a limit on the number of times they can go out each week. They enforce these rules by a fair and consistent punishment for breaking the rules. If a child comes home late, he is "grounded" for a number of evenings or privileges are withheld. That seems to be a disciplinary method "according to the books."

However, that is only one side of the coin. The parents should at the same time, and with no less fervour, encourage desired behaviour. There is the very real danger that staying at home for a number of evenings is equated with punishment. The parents should also show their appreciation when their child comes home early or stays home. They should make staying home more attractive and less of a "must."

We all like to get a pat on the back once in a while. It is rather discouraging for children when they are criticized for their failures, and get punished when they do something wrong, but never get praised or rewarded when they do something right.

We all feel that way. An employee will feel much better, and work harder and with more enthusiasm, when his employer shows his appreciation and praises him once in a while. The pay cheque is important, but a pat on the back is certainly a strong moral incentive and encouragement. The same counts for children. Chores which they do not like too much become easier when they know that it makes their parents happy. The encouragement through a reward is not less important than the discouraging effect of discipline. Such a reward does not necessarily have to be in the form of payment. In most cases, moral encouragement and mental satisfaction should take preference over direct payment. The satisfaction of making someone feel happy can be of equal importance. However, the appreciation has to be shown before it can count as a reward.

There is another aspect we have to be aware of and that is the (sometimes unintentional) rewarding of wrong behaviour. A simple example can illustrate this. If a child, during a church service, is allowed to go to the washroom, it may experience this as a welcome break during a not-too-much appreciated time of sitting still. If the parents do not curtail and discourage this, the child may, even unintentionally, associate it with a nice break. It may happen more often and become a habit which is difficult to get rid of. The same happens when a child ignores or challenges the decision of his parents. If they give in, he is encouraged to try it again.

10. Conclusions

a. The Bible teaches us clearly that discipline is an intrinsic part of childrearing and education. Parents have the duty to teach their children a proper value system. In this teaching corporal punishment takes an important place. It serves to keep them from going in a wrong direction in a world which is infected by the influence of sin. Proverbs 13:24 says: "He who spares the rod hates his son, but he who loves him is diligent to discipline him."

b. All discipline has to be based on loving care, and also obedience to the authorities has to be a matter of love. According to Lord's Day 39 of the Heidelberg Catechism, the fifth commandment requires "that I show honour, love, and faithfulness to my father and mother and all those in authority over me."

c. A child, left to himself, will never develop a proper value system to refer to. Such a child will bring shame to his parents (Prov. 29:15).

d. Two important aspects of discipline are that it has to be fair and consistent. Unfair punishment causes children to lose their respect for the authorities. To explain the meaning and purpose of punishment which children feel is unfair may be necessary. However, this should never take the form of a debate about the correctness of the decision. Inconsistent punishment makes children confused and makes discipline less effective.

e. Discipline is important not only to punish wrongdoing but also to discourage bad behaviour. It should always go together with the encouragement of good behaviour. Every human being likes to be praised and many things are done, not for enjoyment, but for the rewarding results. Rewarding good behaviour works as an incentive and encourages the child to continue in that direction. Unintentionally the result will be associated with the action. The reward and incentive should preferably not be in the form of a "payment" in a direct way but should be the moral or mental satisfaction derived from the action. (cf. Psalm 19:11 and Prov. 11:18.)

f. The main reason for all discipline and for obedience to authorities is the fifth commandment. Lord's Day 39 of the Heidelberg Catechism says that I have to "submit myself with due obedience to their good instruction and discipline, and also have patience with their weaknesses and shortcomings, since it is God's will to govern us by their hand."

g. Let us pray that the Lord may cause the Christian family to remain the prime source of loving discipline and education. Free education is not the ideal; but the beginning of wisdom is the fear of the Lord. Proverbs 29:17 says: "Discipline your son, and he will give you rest; he will give delight to your heart."

22

CHAPTER TWO

The relationship between family and school

1. Parental responsibility

In this chapter I will discuss the relationship between family and school with respect to the responsibility for the children's education. There is one basic rule which we have to honour in all circumstances, and that is that the education of the children and the whole school system is primarily the responsibility of the parents.

We find this basic principle proclaimed already in Deuteronomy 4:10. There we read: "that you may teach your children," and (6:7) "you shall teach your children diligently the commandments of the LORD, and you shall talk with your children when you sit in your house and when you walk by the way."

The Lord has entrusted His children, the children of the covenant, to parents, and He has given them the responsibility to instruct these children in the fear of His Name.

Child rearing is both a privilege and a responsibility. The upbringing of children is not an easy task, but it is a God-given mandate and office. It includes not only the education given at school and in catechism classes, but the complete preparation for their task in this world, in human society, and in the first place for the kingdom of Jesus Christ which is to come.

2. Historical developments

Since earliest times parents have given instruction to their children. The father taught his son how to till the soil and manage the farm. The mother gave instruction to her daughter with respect to housekeeping and cooking.

When society became more complex and education more time-consuming, parents came together to cooperate in setting up an educational system. In this way school societies were born.

Among the people of Israel, and also with the old Greek and Roman people, it was the parents who managed the schools; they had the supervision and the full responsibility.

Later, in the Middle Ages, it was the Christian churches that increasingly became responsible for the schools. They were used by the churches as a tool to christianize the people. That happened at a time when the members of the church no longer saw and accepted their own responsibility. Not only in the matter of the education of the children, but in many other instances as well, the church became the dominating organization.

The clergy had a considerable influence in every area of life, and the so-called "laity" left everything up to the clergy.

Because of the close relationship between the church and the civil government in the thirteenth and the fourteenth century, the school increasingly became a matter of the provincial or federal government. In the sixteenth century, after the great Reformation, the school system was, to a large extent, a governmental matter, and the churches had accepted this situation. The churches used their influence in governmental affairs to assure that education was given in the proper way, that teachers were appointed who were capable of instructing the children not only in reading, writing, arithmetic, and arts, but also in godliness.

In some cases, if necessary, the schools were managed by the deacons or belonged to orphanages, but in most cases they were run by the government.

3. Developments in the Netherlands

Because many Reformed people have their ancestry in Europe, and more particularly in the Netherlands, it might be worthwhile to pay some attention to the developments in that country.

Already the first general synod in the Netherlands after the Reformation, the Synod of Dordrecht 1574, decided that it was the task of the ministers to see to it:

a. that schools should be established by the civil government in all places where they deemed it necessary,

b. that the wages of the teachers should be paid by the government,

c. that the churches should have the opportunity to appoint or select teachers,

d. that the teachers should subscribe to the Confession of Faith,

e. that teachers unwilling to subscribe to the Confession should be dismissed,

f. if the local or provincial government would be unwilling to cooperate in these matters, the minister should appeal these matters in court (Acts, Art. 22).

From these decisions it becomes clear that, though the school system was run by the government, the churches had great influence with respect to both the appointment of teachers and the curriculum. There were some private schools, but also in these school the churches had a certain influence.

The General Synod of Middelburg 1581 decided that officers should be appointed to ensure that the teachers in the schools performed their task in the proper way, and that no errors or heresies would creep in.

Against this background we have to see Article 21 of the Church Order, established at the General Synod of Dordrecht 1618/19. It states: "The consistories everywhere shall see to it that there are good teachers who shall not only teach the children reading, writing, languages, and art, but also instruct them in godliness and the catechism." It is very important to notice that this article was established at a time when:

a. the school system, at least for the better part, was run by the government;

b. the churches had great influence in the matters of the government because of the close relationship between church and civil government;

c. even in private schools, as far as they existed, the churches had great influence, although these schools were not run by the churches as such;

d. a few schools existed which were more or less directly connected with the churches. Those were the schools run by the deacons or the schools annexed to orphanages of the deaconate.

During the French revolution, at the end of the eighteenth century, the situation changed drastically. The ties between church and civil government were either loosened or completely cut. The public school became a tool in the hands of the so-called "neutral" government to indoctrinate the students with revolutionary ideas. It became necessary to establish separate Christian schools, often called "Schools with the Bible," over against the so-called "neutral" public schools.

Some of these schools were established by the initiative of private persons, some were run by the church or by the deaconate.

Because of the ongoing battle against the public school and against the spirit of revolution, it became more and more necessary to get these matters organized better. Therefore school societies were established.

Finally, people had been brought back to the good old Scriptural principle and adage: "The school belongs to the parents." Schools, especially Christian schools, had once again become the responsibility of parents' associations.

As a result of this development arose the question of what the relationship was between the school association and the consistory. Article 21 of the Church Order had been established at a time when the schools were run by the government, while the churches had a great influence in governmental matters and had the opportunity "to see to it" that the instruction was given in a Christian manner.

4. The responsibility of the consistory

As soon as people had gone back to the Biblical rule that education is primarily the responsibility of the parents, many questions arose. Does the consistory have authority over the school society? Does the consistory have any responsibility for what goes on in the school? Do the office-bearers have anything to say in matters of the school society? Does the consistory have oversight only over the members of the congregation, or is also the school system as such subject to the supervision of the consistory?

In this regard there was a difference of opinion between two well-known professors of church polity: Prof. Dr. H. Bouman and Prof. Dr. F. L. Rutgers.

According to Prof. Dr. H. Bouman, consistories also have authority over school societies, and societies of church members can even be subject to the discipline, given by the Lord to the consistory, at least as far as the constitutions of such societies have declared that they accept the Reformed Confession and that they submit themselves to the discipline of the consistory.

Prof. Dr. F. L. Rutgers, on the other hand, pointed out that the consistory has supervision only over the individual members of the congregation, not over societies. The consistory certainly has to see to it that the parents instruct their children according to the Word of God. The consistory may admonish parents when they are unfaithful in this matter. But the consistory does not have any authority or discipline over the school association as such. Only the individual members of the congregation are subject to the authority and discipline of the church. So far the opinion of Prof. Rutgers.

At the General Synod of Leeuwarden 1920 there was a proposal on the table to change Art. 21 of the Church Order and to specify how the consistory is supposed "to see to it that there are good teachers who shall not only teach the children reading, writing, languages, and arts, but also instruct them in godliness and the catechism." General Synod did not accede to this proposal. The report of an advisory committee stated that the consistory certainly has a responsibility with respect to the education of the children and the way they are taught in the school. But the consistory is not supposed to exercise this responsibility by urging these matters on the civil government, as it was done in the sixteenth and seventeenth century, but by making the parents aware of their responsibility.

General Synod decided to emphasize the responsibility of the parents to establish their own schools. As a possibility it mentioned a contract between the school society and the church, allowing the consistory to visit the school to see whether or not the education was given in accordance with the Word of God and the Confession of the Church. General Synod did not deem it necessary to change the Church Order. If interpreted in the right way, the intention of Art. 21 could still be adhered to by the churches.

In the past the Canadian Reformed Churches adopted Article 21 of the Church Order of Dordrecht in its original form. However, with the revision of the Church Order in 1983 also this article was adapted to the present situation in Canada. It has now received a place right after the article dealing with baptism, and reads as follows (Art. 58): "The consistory shall ensure that the parents, to the best of their ability, have their children attend a school where the instruction given is in harmony with the Word of God as the church has summarised it in her Confession." In this way the emphasis and the responsibility is put where it should be.

I will leave it at this as far as the history of this article of the Church Order is concerned. From this historical review at least the following points will be clear:

a. The education of the children and the whole school system is first of all the responsibility of the parents. The school belongs to the parents.

b. The consistory has to see to it that the parents fulfil their task, in accordance with the promise they made at the baptismal font.

c. The old Art. 21 of the Church Order was established at a time when the school system was run by the government, and the intention was to ascertain that the education should be given in a Christian manner.

d. To establish and operate a school is not the task of the consistory. Only in special situations did the churches, or more specifically the deaconate, take the initiative to establish Christan schools, e.g., in orphanages. However, as a rule it has always been the task of the parents.

5. Catechism classes

One aspect of Christian education which needs our special attention is the instruction given in catechism classes. While with the regular school system the responsibility lies with the parents and not with the consistory, with catechism classes it is a different story. This is a type of instruction and education given on behalf of the consistory and under its direct supervision. In the Form for the Ordination of Ministers of the Word the task of the minister is described in four points. Part of his primary duty is: "He shall teach the Word of God to the youth of the church and to others whom God calls, for the Holy Scriptures are able to instruct them for salvation through faith in Jesus Christ." This shows us that the teaching of the youth of the church is not a hobby or a private undertaking of the minister, but part of his primary task as minister of the Word of God.

It is the responsibility of the parents to send their children to catechism classes, but the position of the consistory in this respect is completely different. With respect to the regular school system the consistory has to ensure that the parents, to the best of their ability, have their children attend a school where the instruction is given in harmony with the Word of God as the church has summarised it in her Confession (Art. 58). The consistory has to leave the initiative up to the parents, and the consistory should only get involved when parents are negligent in this respect.

Catechism instruction, however, is the task and the responsibility of the consistory. It is a part, — even one of the most important parts, — of the task of the minister, and the consistory has to support this part of his work and supervise it, taking the full responsibility for it. The members of the consistory are not supposed to visit and sit in on the regular lessons in the elementary and high schools, not even when it is a school closely related to, or solely consisting of, members of the church. The members of the consistory, however, have the right and the duty to stay in touch with the teaching of the youth of the church.

Parents do not only have the responsibility to send their children to these classes, but they even have the duty to cooperate in these matters and give their full support to it. If the parents are negligent, the consistory has to admonish them. Catechism instruction, one of the primary tasks of the minister of the Word, according to the Form for the Ordination, should not be a matter of parental preference or choice; it should be pursued in the proper manner by the whole consistory.

6. Some conclusions

Two things should be clear from what has been said so far, and both are equally important, in my opinion. There are two sides of the same coin.

a. The school is not a neutral matter. It is not true that Christian education is general education plus some religious training. It is not a certain percentage general, neutral education (like reading, writing, arithmatic, science, arts, and physical education) *plus* a certain percentage religion (like Bible, Church History and Catechism). No, the whole school system and the whole curriculum must be Christian. Therefore it is necessary that we have Christian schools wherever possible, under the supervision of the parents. That is one side, and a very important side of the story. But there is also another side, which should not be overlooked.

b. A Christian school is not an extended or glorified catechism class. The task of the school is to equip the children for their task in this world. It has to be done in a Christian manner, but it remains a preparation for their task in this world, in their profession, in their job or in their business. The purpose of catechism classes is to teach the Word of God to the youth of the church, to instruct them for salvation through faith in Jesus Christ (cf. the Form for the Ordination of Ministers of the Word). That is the other side of the coin.

It is important to stress both points, for the following reason: It is the task of the consistory to proclaim the gospel and to take care of the members of the congregation in all spiritual matters. The consistory has to ensure that the members of the congregation, in doctrine and conduct, live according to the Word of God. The consistory must see to it that parents live up to their obligation with respect to the education of their children, that teachers fulfil their task in the proper way, and that the labourer as well as the factory manager are faithful and "carry out the duties of their office and calling as willingly and faithfully as the angels in heaven" (cf. Lord's Day 49 of the Heidelberg Catechism). It is not the task of the consistory, however, to interfere in matters of the school society. That is primarily the task of the parents. The consistory has to make the parents aware of their responsibility. It may even be necessary for the consistory to admonish the parents, because they do not adhere to the promise which they made at the baptismal font.

That is the general rule. It does not mean that there can never be exceptions. Of course, there are. We should not be formalistic. In special situations special measures may be warranted. It is not the primary task of the deacons, for example, to manage an old-age home or hospital. Nevertheless, it has happened in the past on occasion, because it appeared to be necessary. Another example is the mission field. The primary task of a missionary is to preach the gospel, but sometimes missionaries have to help with such things as the construction of an air-strip or the building of a house. A minister is not a social worker in the usual sense of the word, but there are situations in which a minister has to spend a fair amount of his time on cases which usually are dealt with by a social worker.

It is not the task of a consistory to establish a school, but in a particular situation it may be necessary for the consistory to take the initiative, or to communicate with the school society. However, the general rule must be: the school belongs to the parents and it is their primary responsibility.

What holds true for many other cases, holds true for this as well: the more faithful the members of the congregation are in the fulfilment of their task and duty, the less work is left for the consistory.

Let parents fulfil their mandate. May the Lord bless them in their effort to instruct their children and have them instructed "in harmony with the Word of God as the church has summarized it in her Confession."

CHAPTER THREE

The position of adopted children

1. The basic question

The position of adopted children has been a point of discussion in the Reformed Churches in the Netherlands for the last several decades. Even though decisions have been made by general synods, the matter is still not settled. The Canadian Reformed Churches, as far as I am aware, have never made a decision in this respect. In the Reformed Churches in the Netherlands all decisions of general synods since 1892 are considered to be settled and binding, as long as they have not been revoked or changed by a later synod. Although such decisions are not binding for the Canadian Reformed Churches, for situations about which no explicit decision has been made in our country, most people go by what has been decided in the old country.

The matter of baptism of adopted children is a case in point. I have never heard that a consistory denied a request to have an adopted child baptized or that it followed a different route in these matters than the churches on the other side of the ocean.

It is interesting to note that there has been a certain development and shift in the discussion about this issue. At first the attention was focused primarily on the question whether adopted children could be baptized. Slowly, but very clearly, the point has become whether adoption, as such, is acceptable. The question of baptism does not pose a real problem, at least not with those who have an adopted child. Those who use the possibility of adoption as well as those who approve of this option, are usually of the opinion that adopted children ought to be baptized. Those who are opposed to the baptism of adopted children are usually also opposed to adoption per se. They would never adopt a child, for they feel that the whole idea of legal adoption goes too far. They prefer not to go any further than a foster parent relationship in the event that a child has to be placed in another family.

Because of this development in the discussion and this crystalization of opinions, we will deal in this chapter with adoption as such, and leave the question of baptism out of the picture.

We will focus on adoption as such, because not all cases are the same. There certainly are situations in which adoption should not be recommended. There sometimes are wrong motives not only on the part of those who give up a child for adoption but also on the part of those who want to adopt a child. There are also situations in which adoption is the most desirable solution. That is why we want to deal with adoption apart from the question of baptism.

2. Adoption or a foster home?

Different general synods in the Netherlands have busied themselves with questions concerning adoption. In a study report of deputies at General Synod Amersfoort-West 1966/67 adoption was called "a compassionate emergency measure in a sinful world." (Dutch: een barmhartige nood-maatregel in een zondige wereld) (Acts, p. 377).

After lengthy discussions on different aspects of adoption the report comes to the conclusion that "the Lord opens two ways for responsible parenthood and the constitution of a covenant family, namely:
'1. the ordinary way (flesh and blood),
'2. in some cases the extraordinary way of parental compassion (adoption).
'Both ways are governed by His royal good pleasure' " (Acts, p. 381).

In the report of an advisory committee at the same synod we read: "If there is no longer any prospect of a proper functioning of the relationship between parent and child and the unmistakable interest of the child requires a compassionate measure, no objection can be made if the possibility of adoption is utilized. In such a case we are allowed to say that the child, under the guidance of God's providence, has been placed in the foster family" (Acts, p. 508).

These statements of general synod have been discussed extensively for a number of years. A final decision was made by General Synod Hattem 1972. With respect to the question whether it is correct to use the "Adoption Act 1956" for the purpose of adoption synod decided:

"1. That no valid grounds have been brought forward for a general statement that believers are not allowed to make use of the 'Adoption Act.' "

"2. That, if believers submit themselves to the wisdom of the Word of God, they do not have to face any impediment to utilize the 'Adoption Act.' "

We have to notice how carefully synod formulated its statements. It does not say that adoption is *always* the right way to deal with the problem of a child. It does not justify *every* case of adoption. It only says that no grounds have been brought forward for a *general* rejection of *every* form of adoption. It says that the "Adoption Act" *can* be used in the *correct* way. This does not justify or deny the many instances of misuse or abuse of the law.

To understand the crux of the matter it is important to realize what the alternative to adoption is. Adoption means that the child legally becomes a member of the adoptive family. All ties with the natural parents are terminated and the child receives all the rights inherent in being a member of the new family, including the name and the right of inheritance.

The alternative to adoption is the foster home. A foster child does not become a legal member of the family. There is no legal relationship between the child and the foster parents. In some cases, especially with orphans, the foster parents may be given guardianship over the child, but that is not always so. A foster child can easily be moved from one foster home to another, if the guardian so desires, or the child can be returned to the natural parents. In the case of adoption the child becomes a legal child of the adoptive parents. There are only a few, very restricted possibilities to revoke the adoption, and that is always up to the courts.

Because adoption is such a radical measure, with such far-reaching consequences, we will have a closer look at the different implications of it. In what sort of situation is adoption acceptable? What should be the motives of the parents who give up a child for adoption? What should be the motives of the adoptive parents? There certainly can be wrong motives for adoption on both sides, with the natural parents as well as with the adoptive parents. There are situations in which adoption should not be recommended. In what follows I will try to analyze the criteria.

3. The unmistakable interest of the child

In the previous section we saw how general synod emphasized that the unmistakable interest of the child has to be the principal factor in all decisions concerning adoption. Although this may sound obvious, it is too often forgotten or ignored by people who have to deal with cases of adoption.

Many bad feelings about adoption and many protests against adoption are caused by people who use invalid arguments. Why do people want to adopt a child? It is not always in the unmistakable interest of the child. Some want to adopt a child to fill an empty place in their lives, others want to satisfy their desire to have someone to look after and to keep them busy, while still others want to adopt a child because they hope it will bring the joy and happiness in their life which they could not achieve without a child. Their motive is not to show compassion for the child, but to satisfy their own desires, and the result may be that the child does not give the desired "reward." To adopt a child requires self-denial and great sacrifices. There are often unexpected problems and disappointments. If the motive for adoption was the fulfilment of one's own desires, the disappointment may be so great that the adoptive parents give up the child and have it move to another home.

Especially in countries where insufficient legal protection against wrong adoption procedures is provided, there are terrible examples of such shuffling of children.

Adoptive parents should realize, before they start any action, that they have to be prepared to do it only for the unmistakable interest of the child. They have to be prepared to make sacrifices, to cope with unexpected problems, and to face disappointments. They have to bear in mind that the child may turn out to be quite different from what they had expected.

Natural parents can sometimes recognize their own character weaknesses in their children, although they often are in for a surprise: no two children are the same. Even the best-mannered parents can have ill-mannered children. The parent's character and behaviour is not always reflected in the children, although some traits of character, whether good or bad, are often evident in the children. Since adoptive parents usually do not know who the natural parents are, they cannot attribute good or bad characteristics to the parents. Frequently adoptive parents face almost insurmountable problems when the children grow up. That can cause frustration and disappointment and become a matter of great concern. Adoptive parents have to be prepared to face such situations. If they do not begin the whole undertaking out of compassion for the child, they will not be able to cope with such situations.

It is perfectly clear that the family circumstances can be a contributing factor in making a decision to adopt. A childless couple, knowing that they cannot have children of their own, is more likely to consider adoption than a couple with a rapidly growing family. It is also true that adopted children can bring, and have brought, happiness, joy, and the fulfilment of a dream to childless couples. It can be very rewarding and it can give great satisfaction. However, that should never be the main reason for adopting. If compassion for the child is the aim, the parents will be able to cope with the problems and disappointments, and finally find satisfaction and the due reward.

4. Careful consideration on both sides

A decision to give up for adoption or to adopt should never be made without careful consideration. In the previous section we paid some attention to possible motives of adoptive parents. But also the motives of the natural parents or parent must be carefully analyzed. Earlier I quoted from the report of the advisory committee at General Synod Amersfoort-West 1966/67. It stated: "If there is no longer any prospect of a proper functioning of the relationship between parent and child . . . ." That has to be ascertained first. Adoption is a very profound interruption in the life and family relationship of a child. The child is removed from his natural parents. The original relationship is legally terminated and replaced by a completely new and lasting relationship. The child is taken out of its original environment and placed in a new situation. That should only be done if there is no prospect of restoring or improving the natural situation.

A mother should not be pressed to give up her child as long as she is willing and able to take care of the child. The responsibility rests, in the first place, with the natural parent. We might think that a child would be better off, and better cared for, if he were adopted, but let us not forget that the child should be left in his natural situation if at all possible. That, for him, is the best place to be. A child may feel happier there than in a completely different environment where, although he would have more luxury and better care, he still would not feel at home. There have been many disappointments, especially with children from a different part of the world, from a different race, or a different culture. This disappointment can be noticed on both sides: with the adoptive parents as well as with the adopted child.

We have called adoption an "emergency measure in a sinful world" and that is how it should always be considered. If there is no prospect of a proper relationship between parent and child, we have no choice. It can happen that a natural parent is not able to take care of the child.

It also happens that a parent is not willing to take the responsibility. Then we cannot say that the natural relationship between parent and child is disrupted or terminated through adoption. Either there never was such a relationship, or the relationship was broken and destroyed by the parent. In such an emergency situation a compassionate measure has to be taken, in the unmistakable interest of the child, to avoid further damage and suffering on the part of the child.

5. A compassionate emergency measure

We have called adoption a "compassionate emergency measure in a sinful world." There are three aspects to this definition which are equally important and should be taken into consideration in all cases.

a. It has to be a matter of compassion, not selfishness.
b. It has to be an emergency measure, not a standard procedure.
c. We have to realize that we are living in a sinful world.

I have already emphasized the fact that adoption should never take place to satisfy the adoptive parents but only to show mercy to the child. I have also stressed the fact that a decision to give up a child for adoption should not be taken lightly, but only in an emergency situation. The third aspect is equally important. We have to realize that we are living in a sinful world. Adoption should never be seen as an ideal solution and it should never be promoted as an aim in itself. However, in this life we are quite often confronted by the devastating consequences of sin.

While we confess that Jesus Christ came into this world to make full satisfaction for all our sins, the consequences of sin are still felt in this life. Christ, in His care and mercy, uses human beings to alleviate suffering and misery in this life. He showed, during His life on earth, that He cares for those who suffer. He paid special attention to children. He took them into His arms and said, "Let the children come to Me, and do not hinder them; for to such belongs the kingdom of heaven" (Matthew 19:14). And He also said, "Whoever receives such a child in My name receives Me" (Matthew 18:5). He wants to use human beings to help children who need help. He wants us to show mercy and to give relief to children who suffer because of the devastating consequences of their parents' sins.

Giving up a child for adoption is not always a matter of unwillingness on the part of the parent. It is often also a matter of inability to take care of the child. Ninety-five percent of adoptive children come from unwed mothers. Especially in such situations we are confronted by the brokenness of life and the devastating consequences of sin. The mother herself is often still a child and is not able to take care of the baby. Quite often the baby's grandparents do not want to have the child in their house. Either the baby has to leave or both mother and baby are kicked out of the house. They make it impossible for the mother to take care of her baby. This can create an unbearable situation. The young mother can be forced into a situation in which she has only two options, either to give up the child for adoption or to have an abortion. Although a young girl is not necessarily forced into such a dilemma, she often sees it as the only way out.

Because we reject abortion as murder, we have to consider whether adoption can be an acceptable alternative in a situation in which the normal relationship between parent and child is destroyed by sinful human actions. An emergency measure may be necessary in this sinful world, to avoid hurting the victim even more. That does not condone or minimize the sins of the parents and the shortcomings of the grandparents. They have their own responsibilities. However, compassion for the child can make such a measure necessary, to avoid more damage and harm to the child that has become the victim of the wrongdoings of others.

6. Does adoption cut off natural ties?

One of the main objections to adoption is the fact that it cuts off natural ties. The parent-child relationship is terminated by a judicial decision. Do we have the right to terminate or cut off such a relationship or does a judge have the right to do so for that matter? Those who are opposed to adoption argue that a foster home would be an equally effective measure.

We doubt whether this argumentation holds water. If adoption takes place along the lines set out in the previous sections, we cannot really say that a natural relationship is terminated or cut off through adoption. We simply accept the reality that there is no relationship of love and care between the parent and the child. Such a relationship either has never developed or has been destroyed. Legal adoption registers this sad reality.

However, there is more to consider. If a child is placed in a foster home, there is always the possibility for a parent to get the child back. Sometimes a mother, who has given her child up for adoption, wants the child back after he has grown up because she sees a possibility to "exploit" the child. In such a situation legal adoption protects not only the adoptive parents, but first and foremost the child, from being exploited. Also here it is true that adoption should be a measure in the unmistakable interest of the child.

There is another aspect that has to be considered. A child is supposed to obey his parents. After adoption the adoptive parents have become the legal parents and the child knows what he is supposed to do. However, if a child is placed in a foster home, it will usually still have contact with his parents on a more or less regular basis. Such a child is supposed to obey the foster parents while it lives in their house and is under their supervision. However, because the natural parents are still the legal parents, the child also has to obey them. That can, and often does, place the child in the very difficult position of being caught in the middle.

A similar situation arises when parents are involved in divorce proceedings. The child often does not want to make a choice or take sides with the one against the other, but the child still faces a dilemma, because it cannot obey both at the same time. This conflict is even more complicated if one "party" is the real parent and the other "only" a foster parent.

The proper solution in such a situation is to make clear to the child that it has been placed in a new situation. If contacts with the natural parents cause a conflict, in most cases these contacts have to be terminated in the interest of the child. However, that means that, actually, the same situation exists as with legal adoption.

Our conclusion must be that legal adoption is not much different in its effects than a foster home, except that with adoption the factual situation is legally registered and more security is provided for the child, to prevent his unmistakable interest from being ignored to the advantage of those who want to exploit him.

7. The possibility of repentance

We have stated before that adoption can be necessary because of the brokenness of human life, as a consequence of sin. Some argue that adoption is too radical a measure because it is irreversible. It does not leave enough room for repentance and the restoration of the original situation after amendment of life. That sounds reasonable and is certainly a point to be considered carefully. However, there are a few aspects we should take into consideration as well.

Before the court grants a request for legal adoption, the child has to be in a foster home for a certain period of time. The court decides whether it is in the unmistakable interest of the child to continue that situation. Before it comes to a formal adoption the child has already gone through a lot of embarrassment and suffering. After a while the child begins to feel at home and gets used to the new situation. A new relationship of love, trust, and care is growing. The child sees the foster parents or the adoptive parents as the people who care for him and love him. The child feels safe and protected in his new environment. That is the actual situation. It may have been caused by the sinful attitude of the natural parents, or by their negligence or unwillingness to take care of the child. In any event, it is a matter of fact that the child, after much suffering, finally has found a safe place to live. The child is settled in a new environment. To remove him from his new home and bring him back to his natural parents will usually only cause more embarrassment and suffering.

It is very well possible that the parents, after a number of years, recognize the mistake they have made and ask for forgiveness. We always should be prepared to forgive. But to confess a sin does not take away the consequences of such a sin, and real repentance and remorse have to be shown also in the way someone accepts and carries the burden of lasting consequences of his wrongdoings. Trying to put the burden of one's wrongdoings on someone else is not a proof of real repentance. Neither is it correct to ignore, minimize, or deny the consequences of one's own specific sins.

If a drunken driver kills someone in a traffic accident, he may ask for forgiveness, and we have to be prepared to forgive, but that does not take away the fact that he has to face justice in court, nor does it bring back the person who has been killed. When a parent has destroyed the relationship of love, respect, and trust between parent and child, and later confesses his or her sin and asks forgiveness, we have to forgive, but that does not take away the fact that the parent-child relationship has been destroyed. A new relationship may grow, but it would be wrong to expect the child to act as if nothing had happened. That would put the burden of the consequences of the wrongdoing on the child instead of on the parent who was in the wrong. If a parent, for whatever reason, treats a child in such a way that it has to be placed in a foster home or in an adoptive family, the relationship of love, trust, and affection between parent and child is damaged, destroyed, or prevented from developing. Real repentance in such a situation means accepting this reality as a consequence of one's own previous actions. It might be hard for the parent to accept the fact that the child is placed in another family, but requiring the child to come back is not a proof of real remorse and willingness to make up for previous wrongdoings. Instead it means that extra suffering is imposed upon the child to give the parent the feeling that the past has been undone. It is an attempt to exonerate the parent at the cost of the child. It is like cutting down a tree and, having apologized for it, demanding the fruits of the tree.

Remorseful parents should show how real their repentance is by leaving the child in the new situation. They first have to consider the unmistakable interest of the child. Their own feelings and emotions come second. That might be the sacrifice required to make up for the past.

For all these reasons I do not believe that adoption ignores the possibility of repentance on the part of the negligent parent. It only protects the child against unreasonable demands of parents who want to let their child pay and carry the burden of their own wrongs.

8. Abuse of adoption

Objections to adoption are sometimes triggered by cases in which the possibility of legal adoption is abused. I have heard about tragic and heartbreaking cases. Some parents "buy" a child to fulfil their own dreams. In some countries there seems to be a "black market" for children. The poverty and misery of people is abused. Children are sold and smuggled out of the country illegally. With false papers they are given up for adoption. Unscrupulous people are making money this way.

As I have stated before, adoption always has to be a well-considered decision, in the unmistakable interest of the child. It has to be a compassionate measure. Many cases in which a child is "bought" only to satisfy the adoptive parents, turn sour. The child becomes the victim of disappointment on the part of the adoptive parents -- a disappointment which is the result of wrong expectations.

We have to emphasize, time and again, that the first responsibility for the child lies with the natural parents. Adoption should only be considered if there is no prospect of a proper functioning of the relationship between parent and child. It should be an emergency measure in the unmistakable interest of the child.

Abuse of adoption should not drive us to the other extreme of condemning every good application of this possibility. Legal adoption is a measure to avoid such abuse. The courts have to decide whether the interest of the child is really served by adoption. It should be a matter of mercy. We know that "the mercy of the wicked is cruel" (Proverbs 12:10), but we as Christians have to show what compassion and mercy really mean. It has to be the mercy taught by Holy Scripture. Jesus Christ showed us what real mercy is. He showed compassion for children, and we have to follow His example. He laid His hands on them and said, "Let the children come to Me, and do not hinder them; for to such belongs the kingdom of heaven"; and, "Whoever receives such a child in My name receives Me."

In order to avoid abuse of adoption we have to consider all aspects and be on the alert. The support and guidance of the office-bearers is necessary in a case of adoption. However, that requires some knowledge on the part of the office-bearer of the implications and the ethical aspects of adoption. It happens, too often, that the adoption of a child occurs without any involvement, advice, or support from the office-bearers. They get involved after the whole matter has been settled and baptism of the child is requested. Office-bearers, stay in touch with the families, also in this respect. Families, ask the advice and support of your office-bearers.

9. God's sovereign good pleasure

There is still one very important point that needs attention. Some argue that a husband and wife who have no children and know that they cannot have children of their own, have to accept the sovereign good pleasure of the Lord in their life also in this respect. Isn't adoption an attempt to go against what the Lord has brought into their life or has kept away from them? Should they not accept the will of the Lord in their life, rather than try to constitute a family through adoption? These seem to be relevant and legitimate questions and very suggestive ones at that. However, I consider these questions more suggestive than convincing. Of course, we all have to accept the Lord's sovereign good pleasure. However, that does not mean that we have to sit idle and accept a certain situation as being unavoidable if we are able to make a change for the better. We have our own responsibility and we are allowed to use the available means. When we are sick, we have to accept the sovereign good pleasure of the Lord. With an incurable illness, we have to see the hand of the Lord, and we can count on His help to cope with the problems. We know and confess that He will turn everything to our benefit. Our heavenly Father takes care of us and He never makes a mistake. And yet, when we are sick, we have to see a doctor and make use of the available means to cure the disease. A person who refuses to see a doctor should not speak about the sovereign good pleasure of the Lord but confess his own negligence and irresponsibility. We have to accept our responsibility and we have to give account to the Lord for what we have done with the available means.

If a young couple, after having been married for a number of years, still has no children, they may see a doctor to find out whether there is a specific reason and whether something can be done to take away the cause of the apparent infertility. In some cases there is a simple remedy. In other cases more complicated measures are required. It may be necessary to perform an operation to take away an obstacle. In any case the people do not sit idle and say that it is the sovereign good pleasure of the Lord. No, they try to solve the problem, within the scope of their responsibilities and possibilities. This is certainly not in conflict with accepting God's sovereign good pleasure. This counts for all medical treatment.

When a couple comes to the conclusion that they cannot have children of their own, or that it is very unlikely, are they allowed to apply for adoption to constitute a (larger) family in this way, or do they have to accept their childless family as the will of God with respect to their life?

The answer depends on the circumstances and the motives for their actions. I have already explained that adoption should never be initiated to fulfil one's own wishes or to satisfy one's own desires. However, it is very well possible that the Lord wants to use a childless couple to show mercy to a child that needs help and to provide a new home for it. That can also be seen as the sovereign good pleasure of the Lord. The main question is whether such a decision is made in prayer, expecting the help, wisdom and guidance of the Lord, and in a desire to serve Him.

Adoption is an unusual way to receive a child. It should remain an emergency measure. But adoptive parents who go this way in prayer because they feel it is their God-given task, are certainly allowed to see the sovereign good pleasure of the Lord in it. They may consider it a privilege to be allowed to show mercy through this compassionate provision in a sinful world. They can accept such a child as a gift from the hand of the Lord. If they are prepared, in self-denial and with many sacrifices, to take care of a child that needs help, they will probably enjoy the satisfaction of being allowed to bring up a child in the fear of the Lord.

I will conclude with a quote taken from the report at General Synod Hattem 1972 (p. 532). "We certainly do not have to speak about the sovereign good pleasure of the Lord only in a case where a couple remains without children. We can be equally convinced of, and confess, the sovereign good pleasure of the Lord if it pleases Him to give children via this measure of child protection."

CHAPTER FOUR

The position of handicapped children

1. A selfish society

In the previous chapters we paid attention to different aspects of family life. We discussed the matter of having children, adopting children, and raising children. It was pointed out that tender loving care has to be shown to children and that love must determine the relationship with them. Such love does not contradict discipline, but, most importantly, it involves care for the other and a willingness to bring sacrifices of self-denial. This important side of family life is a rare commodity today.

We live in a selfish society. Everything is geared to efficiency. We are accustomed to throwaway items in every area of life. We discard everything that does not serve a purpose or is not worth being maintained or repaired. This trend can be noticed even with respect to human life. Old, demented, and useless people, and those who have become a burden to society, have to be discarded by means of euthanasia. Little ones who do not fit into the program, who are unwelcome, have to be destroyed either before, or shortly after, birth.

In this chapter I will not deal with abortion in general, but I would like to pay attention to the position of special children and our attitude towards them. The expression "special children" in this context refers to those who are different because of physical or mental deficiencies. They are also called the "handicapped."

Prenatal care has drastically increased during the last decades. All kinds of tests can be performed before a baby is born to determine whether the child is healthy or suffers some anomalies. These tests are very important, but there is also a danger involved, and caution is certainly required.

Such tests can be necessary to determine whether special measures have to be taken to protect the health of either the baby or the mother. It can even be a "life-saving" matter. Sometimes labour has to be induced at an early stage or a caesarean section has to be performed to save the life of the baby or to prevent further complications or worsening of an existing condition. In all such cases prenatal tests are of great help. They can provide vital information.

However, there is also a dangerous aspect of which we should be aware. Some tests are performed to determine whether a child should be aborted or not. When a child suffers certain defects, especially a physical or mental handicap *which cannot be cured*, abortion may be recommended. That can happen in cases of Down's Syndrome, spina bifida or other serious defects. Down's Syndrome, also called mongolism, causes severe retardation. Spina bifida is a defective closure of the spine, which can cause serious damage to the spinal cord, paralysis, and other severe problems. In such cases a prenatal test incurs the danger that a not-so-scrupulous doctor will advise his patient to have an abortion. In the case of mongolism nothing can be done to change the situation, and therefore it does not serve any purpose to let the mother know in advance that her baby suffers from this disease. In the case of spina bifida a prenatal test can provide information to suggest the need for caesarean section, preventing unnecessary aggravation of the defect during delivery.

The main point in all these cases is that we also have to accept special children, with their mental or physical abnormalities, as human beings, created by the Lord, intricately wrought by His Fatherly hand, and of no less value than others.

In what follows we will determine what our attitude has to be towards such special children and their parents. We often take it for granted that healthy children are born, but every birth is a wonder of God's creating power. To watch such a delicate creature always makes one wonder how people dare to destroy such a work of God's almighty hand by their cruel tools of abortion. It also makes one wonder how it is possible that such a child is so perfectly and intricately wrought by the Lord (cf. Psalm 139:15). We should certainly not take it for granted that a child is healthy. Those who have been confronted with "special children" realize what it means.

Now we have to face the question how we approach such children and their parents. Are such children a burden we have to live with? Are the parents to be pitied for their unfortunate circumstances? Or do we consider also these children to be a blessing? Do they have an important place in human life and do they serve a purpose? In what follows we will see that they certainly are not less important than "normal" children. They are very valuable and precious indeed.

2. How precious they are!

There are a lot of misconceptions among outsiders about the value and meaning of special children, and about the way parents feel and cope with their problems. Some consider these children only as poor pitiable creatures, and the parents unfortunate people who have to put up with an almost unbearable problem.

Now no one can deny that such parents have a difficult task and that they certainly, on occasion, feel sad about their circumstances. However, more has to be said to give a balanced view about their situation.

When we deal with such families, it is always a surprise to note that they see their special child in the first place as their precious child and not as a poor wretch. They enjoy all kinds of little things. They overlook the handicap. It is their child, a child that provides them with lots of joy, happiness, and unity in the family.

When you deal regularly with such children, you learn to see through their being different, and you learn to appreciate their personality. It is certainly not always, and not only, a burden. Consider also how often a "normal" child can cause problems, discord and frustration in a family. It is remarkable to see how such normal children can cause a lot of trouble and disunity, while these special children often promote an atmosphere of unity, closeness, happiness and peace.

I have had the privilege of visiting different summer camps of physically and mentally handicapped children, as well as special "catechism classes" or "Bible classes" for these children. There are few things I have enjoyed more than the openness, honesty, thankfulness and happiness of such children. With normal adults and children you always have to be on your guard. They can fool you, pretending something which is not real. Although special children can react in an unusual way and express themselves in an unexpected manner, they are often more honest and straightforward than many "normal" people. When a Bible story is told they can ask questions which give food for thought, and they can express their feelings and their faith in a way which makes you feel ashamed.

Dealing with such children I have often been reminded of the words of our Lord Jesus Christ, mentioned in Matthew 19:14, "Let the children come to Me, and do not hinder them; for to such belongs the kingdom of heaven," and in Matthew 18:3,4, "Truly I say to you, unless you turn and become like children, you will never enter the kingdom of heaven. Whoever humbles himself like this child, he is the greatest in the kingdom of heaven."

3. Special treatment

Another aspect of this matter is the question how we have to treat such children and their parents. Do they need to be pitied and treated in a special way? A general guideline is that few people like it to be singled out. Handicapped people, adults as well as children, and the parents of handicapped children, want to be, and should be, treated as normally as possible. Don't systematically avoid speaking about that fact of life, but don't overdo it either. People like to be treated normally. They want you to show interest in their child, his weal and woe, his progress, and how nice and special he is to them. But they also want to be treated as normal parents and they don't want too much pity.

Also the handicapped person himself, whether he is a child or an adult, has to be treated as normally as possible. You should not ignore a physical handicap, but do not overemphasize it either. A handicapped person sometimes needs assistance. Such help should be given in a natural way, but don't take everything out of his hands. A person's self-esteem is boosted by showing that he can manage without help. Even if it takes him some extra time and effort, don't be too hasty to take over.

With respect to mentally handicapped or retarded persons, we have to be careful not to act or to speak in a childish way. Some people tend to use childish language. Keep in mind that retarded children, although they might not be able to express themselves normally, can understand you much better if you use normal language. Moreover, how can they ever learn to use proper phrases, if everyone speaks to them in a childish way? They often understand more than we are aware of, although they are not always able to show it by a proper response.

A question that has been discussed in many places and at different levels is whether special church services should be held for mentally handicapped children, or whether they should participate in the normal services. Some people even wonder whether they should participate in the worship service at all, because they cannot understand it anyway. As in many similar situations, the answer cannot be reduced to a plain yes or no. They certainly belong to the congregation as children of the covenant, no less than other children. They should participate in congregational life as much as possible. Even when they cannot understand everything and do not always behave like others, they should be included as much as possible. They probably enjoy it more than we are aware of, and being together with the congregation may mean more for them than for many a smart child or adult who does not pay much attention or sleeps all the time.

In general, I am not in favour of special services for such children. We should try to pay attention to them in the regular services, if need be, and if the circumstances permit. A few words can mean a lot to them. They sometimes hear, feel, and understand more than we realize.

Once I preached in a congregation where a group of handicapped children were present. They had a summer camp in that area, and a row of children in wheelchairs was sitting at the front of the congregation. I had a sermon on Ephesians 4:20. In Dutch it says: "Gij geheel anders" (You completely different). It was a hot summer day. All the elders had taken off their jackets and had walked in, dressed in their white shirts. A retarded boy in a wheelchair was playing with a piece of paper and a pencil. After the service he showed one of the leaders of the summer camp his piece of paper. On it was a row of men, one of them black and all the others white. He had noticed that only the minister wore a black jacket, and he had made his own application of the text. It was certainly not the most appropriate application of the text, but it showed at least that he had heard the text and that he had noticed what was going on. Such children certainly hear, see, and feel much more than we think.

Although I am not in favour of excluding such children from a regular church service by introducing special services for them, I strongly endorse having special Bible classes for them or giving them special instruction in another way, adjusted to their level of comprehension. That brings us to our next point: how we use the talents which the Lord has entrusted to us.

4. Using the talents

In Matthew 25 we find a sermon of our Lord Jesus Christ about the kingdom of heaven and the day of judgment. Three parables are used to show us what the most important things are. First we find the parable of the ten maidens to show us that we always have to be on the alert. The second is the parable of the talents, showing us that we will be judged according to what we have done with the talents which have been entrusted to us. The more talents given to us, the greater is our responsibility. The third parable shows us what will count in the day of judgment, namely, what our attitude has been, not in the first place with respect to great things, but first and foremost in our dealings with our brothers and sisters. "Truly, I say to you, as you did it to the least of these My brethren, you did it to Me" (verse 40).

With respect to our topic we can learn at least two things from this chapter. In the first place, it is of utmost importance how we deal with these seemingly unimportant members of the church, these "least of the brethren." Even a cup of water given to them, a visit, or a little proof of attention to them, can be so significant that it will be mentioned on the great day when the Son of Man comes in His glory, and all His angels with Him, to sit on His glorious throne (Matthew 25:31-46). This chapter also shows us that we will be judged, not according to how many talents we have received, but according to what we have done with the talents entrusted to us.

In Matthew 21:31 Jesus warns the chief priests and the elders of the people, saying, "Truly, I say to you, the tax collectors and harlots go into the kingdom of God before you." That was a harsh statement to people who felt that they were the "creme de la creme" of the people. They thought they would be the first to go into the kingdom of God. Needless to say, they were very upset because of this admonition of our supreme Teacher.

Sometimes I wonder how many retarded or other handicapped children will enter the kingdom of God before highly regarded and self-confident members of the church. Handicapped children may sometimes act in an unusual way and they certainly do not understand everything — sometimes only a little — about the things which we consider to be very important. But they are often more honest and more straightforward. They do not put up a front. Many intelligent people pretend to be something they are not. They talk very nicely, but behind your back they are different. Also in the church there is a lot of disappointment and frustration because of people who deceive one another.

Retarded children do not have many talents. In dealing with them we also notice that sin does not leave any life untouched. But let us not disregard these children. They are members of the covenant no less than the intelligent ones. They belong to the congregation and they have their place in the kingdom of God no less than the others. That may be a comfort for the parents as well as for the children. In Matthew 19:13-15 we read how the disciples tried to keep children away from Jesus, but how He laid His hand on them and blessed them, saying to the disciples, "Let the children come to Me, and do not hinder them; for to such belongs the kingdom of heaven." We are fully aware of the fact that this text does not speak specifically about retarded or other mentally handicapped children, but it shows us that children belong to the kingdom of heaven no less than adults, and that applies also to special children. When the disciples were arguing about the question who was to be considered the greatest among them, Jesus taught them a lesson. He put a child in the midst of them and said, "Truly, I say to you, unless you turn and become like children, you will never enter the kingdom of heaven. Whoever humbles himself like this child, he is the greatest in the kingdom of heaven."

Let us take to heart this warning, and let us also remember what the apostle Paul says in I Corinthians 9. We have to use all the gifts, the talents, and the energy which the Lord has given us, in the same way as a runner who competes in a race. Only the Lord knows whether we have used all our talents in the proper way, and whether we have run and competed in an honest way. Paul himself says in I Corinthians 9:26,27: "I pommel my body and subdue it, lest after preaching to others I myself should be disqualified."

5. Bear one another's burdens

In Galatians 6:2,3 Paul says, "Bear one another's burdens, and so fulfil the law of Christ. For if one thinks he is something, when he is nothing, he deceives himself." As members of the church, members of the same body, the body of Christ, we have to help and to support each other. That counts in a special way when it comes to handicapped children and their parents. The important question is: How can we give such help and support in the most appropriate way? How can we bear another's burdens and so fulfil the law of Christ?

I have already mentioned that we should treat such people as normally as possible. We should not single them out. Of course, we have to acknowledge that they have special problems, and we should not avoid speaking about it. But we have to realize also that such parents have their pride. They don't see their child only as a poor pitiable creature. Their child gives them a lot of joy and happiness, and they are proud of what he is able to do in spite of his handicap. Their child is a fullfledged member of the communion of saints. It certainly causes concerns, but let us not forget that "normal" and very intelligent children can cause problems which often are more difficult to cope with than caring for a handicapped child.

One who has had the opportunity to watch the family situation closely will admit that the life of such a special child makes sense and serves a purpose. Many a mentally handicapped child has been of more value for his environment, a greater blessing for his family, and of more significance for the kingdom of heaven, than some highly regarded and intelligent people who pretend to be something they aren't.

6. Public profession of faith

The last point I would like to touch on is the question in how far mentally handicapped children can make public profession of faith and take part in the celebration of the Lord's Supper. A number of aspects have to be considered in this respect.

In the first place we have to realize that the Lord has given two different sacraments. In baptism the Lord gives a sign and seal of His promises to the children of believers, "without their knowledge" (see Form for

Baptism of Infants). In the Lord's Supper the believers are expected to participate actively in remembering the death of the Lord. Jesus said (according to I Corinthians 11:24,26): "Do this in remembrance of Me," and "as often as you eat this bread and drink the cup, you proclaim the Lord's death until He comes." Participation in the celebration of the Lord's Supper requires some knowledge and understanding, to "discern the body" (I Corinthians 11:29). Before someone can make public profession of faith and sit at the table of the Lord, it has to be shown that the person has at least some understanding of what it means.

In the second place we have to realize that the Lord has given us this sacrament to strengthen our faith, but that He can work with His grace and Holy Spirit also without the use of this sacrament. That is a comfort for those who, by reason of persecution, cannot celebrate the Lord's Supper. It is a comfort also for those who, because of illness, cannot attend the church services. We have to use the sacraments when we are able to, but the Lord can work also without these means.

In the situation of the mentally handicapped it means that the Lord can work in their hearts and minds even when they are not able to take part in the celebration of the Lord's Supper. The fulfillment of the covenant promises does not depend on how smart we are, but on how faithfully we use the talents He has given us, no matter how residual these talents may be.

In the Canons of Dort, Chapter I, Article 17, we read: "We must judge concerning the will of God from His Word, which declares that the children of believers are holy, not in nature but by virtue of the covenant of grace, in which they are included with their parents. Therefore, God-fearing parents ought not to doubt the election and salvation of their children whom God calls out of this life in their infancy." We confess that the Lord can fulfil His promises, even when a child dies before it is born and when it never has had any opportunity to accept or reject His promises. Would the Lord not be able to save children who are so severely retarded that they cannot understand what the covenant means?

At the same time we have to be aware of the fact that public profession of faith requires knowledge, according to the talents one has received. A very intelligent student, with excellent marks in high school, has to show knowledge of Holy Scripture and of the Confession of the church, according to his capability. The armour of God in his situation has to be aimed at a profound attack of the devil during his further study and in his career. I remember cases of less educated, simple people, who at an old age joined the church. No one would expect them to learn the whole Heidelberg Catechism by heart. A very basic testimony about their trust in the Lord is sufficient. The same applies to retarded and other mentally handicapped children. No one can expect them to learn large sections of the Catechism by heart. I have seen retarded children confess their faith in a very simple way. However, a basic understanding is required. They should realize what they are doing. If children do not have the slightest notion of what the Lord's Supper is all about, they should not be admitted to the table of the Lord. Jesus has said, "Do this in remembrance of Me,"

and the apostle Paul says, "as often as you eat this bread and drink the cup, you proclaim the Lord's death until He comes." Those who do not have the slightest understanding of what it means, cannot take part in it. That does not mean that they are not partakers of Christ and all His benefits. The promise, signed and sealed in baptism, stands. It is for them no less than for the children, referred to in the Canons of Dort, I, 17.

Let us not disregard these members, who may seem to be the least of our brothers and sisters, but who may turn out to be the greatest in the kingdom of God.

CHAPTER FIVE

The position of elderly people

1. A forgotten group?

In the previous chapters we discussed the position of adopted children as well as handicapped ones. In this chapter we will focus on another group, namely, the elderly. What is their position in our midst, and how do we deal with them? Do we show due respect to the elderly, or do we only tolerate them? Do they still have a task and place in daily life, or have they become spectators, standing or sitting on the sidelines? How do we treat our elderly members and how do we take care of them? Is an old age home with nursing facilities the ideal situation or do we prefer to have them in a normal family setting? And what do they themselves prefer? In the past the older generation used to live with their children and grandchildren. Nowadays the situation is different. Is that an improvement or is it only for the convenience of an overly busy new generation? Such questions become even more pressing when we deal with demented persons.

We live in the era of the youth. In the past the younger generation had to learn a trade or skill from the older generation. In the guilds the younger generation was painstakingly taught the secrets of the trade by the older members. Nowadays it is different. Modern technology has resulted in a rapidly changing society. Children play and grow up with computers, and many students outsmart their teachers in computer literacy. Recently I heard on the news that a group of high school students was able to "break" the security code of an important institution. They were invited to test the system and within seven minutes they managed to get through a security system which was considered to be "safe." While many older people have no idea what a computer is, children today grow up with it; it is part of their lives, in their games as well as in their education. This development makes elderly people feel even more alienated. Their experience, their skills and their knowledge, which were such vital elements in the guilds in the past, seem to be of no value any longer.

In order to put matters in the right perspective, we had better first listen to what the Bible says about the position of the elderly.

2. What does the Bible say?

The Bible very often speaks about the elders of the people. When this expression is used, especially in the Old Testament, it has a dual meaning. The "elders of the people" refers to a certain group of officers who were in charge of ruling and governing the people. At the same time the title "elders" indicates that older and more experienced people were chosen for this office. Age was considered very important, and the difference in age between two persons counted as a guideline to determine their position with respect to each other. In the book of Job we read about four friends of Job's who came to comfort him and to admonish him. One of them, named Elihu, was apparently rather young, compared to the others. Therefore he waited and listened until the others had finished their speeches. After the other three had spoken a few times, and after Job had answered them, he, the youngest one, finally spoke. In Job 32:6,7, we read, "And Elihu the son of Barachel the Buzite answered: 'I am young in years, and you are aged; therefore I was timid and afraid to declare my opinion to you. I said, 'Let days speak, and many years teach wisdom.' " In this particular case wisdom was not synonymous with age. Elihu was disappointed with what his older friends had said. Therefore we read in verses 8-10, "But it is the spirit in a man, the breath of the Almighty, that makes him understand. It is not the old that are wise, nor the aged that understand what is right. Therefore I say, 'Listen to me; let me also declare my opinion.' " Although in this particular situation the words of Job's youngest friend showed more wisdom than what was said by the three older men, it still shows us the respect he had for the aged. It also demonstrates that, in general, the opinion of older people was considered to be very important.

The fifth commandment says that we have to honour our father and our mother and all those who are in authority over us. In I Timothy 4:12 the apostle Paul encourages the (apparently rather young) preacher and office-bearer Timothy, saying, "Let no one despise your youth." This text shows us that an office-bearer does not necessarily have to be an older man. Still in general, age is considered important. Even today, in many local regulations for the election of office-bearers, we find the rule that in case of a tie vote the older of the two is considered to be chosen.

The Bible teaches us clearly that we have to respect and honour older people because of their age. Real wisdom is often not a matter of study and academic standing, but rather of experience in the school of life, in which many things have to be learned the hard way in the course of the years. The Bible also teaches us that the elderly ought to give wise judgment, but that age is not a guarantee for being right, as the example of Job 32:6-10 shows.

These are the basic rules which we should keep in mind when we have a closer look at the position of the elderly people.

3. Remaining involved

One of the most important aspects of the position of the elderly is that they should remain involved in social life as much as possible. In most jobs and professions there is a mandatory retirement age. Retirement is a very important point in the life of elderly people. It often means a complete change in their pattern of life. Especially for people who have no hobbies or other activities which keep them busy, it can be a dangerous transition. All of a sudden they feel useless, put aside. In many instances we see that such people have problems with their health, while they never had such problems before. One's mental and physical conditions are so closely related that such a drastic change is reflected in both. It would be going too far to advocate doing away with a mandatory retirement age, as some propagate. Although some might very well be able to continue past such an age, others are happy that they can enjoy a well-deserved rest, without being outrightly declared disabled. There is certainly a great difference in personal circumstances. A mandatory retirement age is useful. Without it some might not be willing to give up; they would continue even when they are physically not able to do so, or while the quality of their work or their production goes down. Besides, with the current high unemployment rate it is advisable to give younger people a chance to find a job.

The most important point in this respect is that retirement does not mean that someone becomes useless. Certainly not. However, one must prepare himself well in advance for such a change in one's way of life. Retirement means that someone is relieved from his regular duties, and that he can spend time on other things. Older people should remain involved in everyday life as much as possible. There is a lot of so-called "unpaid" work, that can be done. Such a transition cannot be made overnight, but requires careful preparation. It is remarkable to see how many people start having health problems shortly after they retire, while those who have adapted to their new situation are less prone to suffer such a "transition syndrome."

It is certainly not true that older people cannot make an important contribution to community life. Not everyone can be active in the same way. That is why retirement opens the possibility to adjust to a person's own capabilities. There are cases where people at an older age started an important career. Some have become Head of State or President at an age when others retire. Recent examples can be found in the United States, France and Germany. Others have managed to obtain a doctor's degree after retirement. However, those are the exceptions. Most people have to slow down, but can still be of great value while they are retired. The worst thing is to "give up" and sit idle. That is true in a lot of circumstances, but in a special way for the elderly. They should try to remain involved in everyday life, and the younger generation should give them the opportunity to remain involved and stimulate them to be active, within the limitations of their position. The younger generation can certainly gain a lot by using the experience and the wisdom of the older generation. Let us not ignore the Biblical guideline. Although it might seem outdated, the advice of Job 32:7 is still relevant. "Let days speak, and many years teach wisdom."

4. The problem of stepping down

After what has been said in the previous section about the importance of remaining involved, we also have to pay attention to the other side of the coin, the problem of stepping down when necessary. In almost every position in human society there comes a time when someone cannot function any longer at an optimum level, or even in a reasonably sufficient way. It is always difficult to acknowledge that one has to step down or give up a certain position. Everyone has his pride, and it almost seems to be a matter of capitulation, to acknowledge that someone else has to take over the job. However, it can be a proof of wisdom to step down, to slow down, or to hand over a task to the younger generation. Once I heard someone giving this advice to his middle-aged colleagues: "Try to step down before others have to ask you to step aside." Although it is not always easy to give up something, we should realize that others might be better equipped to take over, while for the person who gives up a certain task, something else may be available that fits his qualifications much better. A Christian, especially, should realize that the Lord did not only give different talents to different people, but that He also asks from us to use our gifts in the way He requires. Unwillingness to give up, to step down, or to take up another task, is certainly not the most appropriate attitude for a Christian.

5. Taking care of the elderly

Care for the elderly is becoming more and more of a problem, for a variety of reasons. The combination of better health care and the subsequently increasing average lifespan, and the declining birthrate, cause very specific problems. In the future there will be an increasing number of elderly to take care of, and an equally decreasing number of people to provide and pay for the facilities to take care of them. In the time of the Old Testament the older generation was always in the centre of attention and was highly respected by all. It was not too long ago that even in our modern society older people stayed with their relatives as much as possible, and only in exceptional cases were transferred to an old age home. Such old age homes were not nice facilities. They were for the poor, the demented and those who did not have any relative to look after them. Such homes were run either by the deacons or by the government. In those homes the elderly had little or no privacy. I still remember the homes with one bedroom for eight or more women and another bedroom for the same number of men, with married couples separated from each other because of lack of privacy. They sometimes certainly lived in deplorable circumstances.

Nowadays we have very nice, comfortable facilities for the elderly. However, care for those who need help, the physically dependent and the demented, is still a problem. The costs are high and usually cannot be paid by the elderly themselves. Their relatives are often not able to pay for such expensive facilities either. The budgets of the nursing homes are lowered. The reduced staff is under constant pressure. They do not have enough time to pay sufficient attention to the elderly who completely depend on their help. A recent report of the CLAC about the working and living conditions in Ontario Nursing Homes revealed that most nursing homes are seriously understaffed and underfunded. Budgets needs to be doubled to provide adequate care. By way of comparison the report mentions the fact "that our society spends more than $ 120 a day per prisoner and less than $26 a day per elderly, disabled nursing home resident."

In the Netherlands the question whether government help can be accepted for the housing of elderly or whether this should be paid for by the deacons has been a topic of discussion for years. Nowadays almost everywhere in the Netherlands old age homes as well as nursing homes are heavily subsidized or completely paid for by the government. In Canada the government is less eager to pick up the tab. That makes the question whether we should move the elderly to a special home or whether we should try to take care of them in a family setting more urgent.

6. Special facilities for the elderly

Earlier we saw that the question whether elderly people have to step down or remain involved in all kinds of activities is not a clear-cut matter. It can be a proof of wisdom that an elderly person gives up a certain job and hands it over to a member of the younger generation, in order to be able to carry on with other activities or to take up a more suitable task. In some instances, however, it might be better to let the older person carry on, instead of giving him the feeling that he is finished. It all depends on the circumstances. No two cases are the same. We have to find the right balance. Some people have to slow down in time, in order to be able to remain involved in a position they can still handle.

The same is true, to a certain extent, regarding the housing of elderly people. The right balance has to be found. What does that mean? Let me try to explain.

Some elderly couples live in their own homes, and are quite capable of taking care of themselves. Age is not the determinant. Whether they still can manage their own household depends on their physical and mental condition. If a couple does not need any help and is able to take care of everything, it would be foolish to force them to leave their familiar environment and to move them into an old age home, where they would have only a small apartment. It would restrict freedom and force them to sit on the sidelines.

Another couple, possibly of the same age or even younger, may come into a situation in which it is very difficult for them to take care of everything. Their house becomes too big for them, and too much work is required to keep it up. In such a situation help is needed. It is nice if children, living close by, are able to provide the necessary help. It might be better, though, for them to move into a senior citizens home, where they have less room, but are able to manage without help. False pride should not prevent them from giving up an existing situation which has become too much for them, in order to accept a less demanding, but in the long run more satisfying position.

Another situation in which the right balance has to be found arises when people become either physically dependent or emotionally disturbed or demented. It is nice when older people, especially those who are widowed, can stay with their children and be cared for in the family setting. We should not be too eager to put them away in an institution. The situation in a nursing home is often far from ideal, especially in the present situation of restraint and understaffing. If there is a real possibility to stay home, it certainly is to be preferred. However, we also have to realize that in many situations it is almost impossible to keep up the good work. False pride should not prevent people from accepting the help of a nursing home in cases where it is really warranted.

It is very important to ensure that we do not forget those who are placed in a special home. The saying, "out of sight, out of mind," should not apply to such situations. Nursing home residents often very eagerly look forward to a visit or some other proof of attention.

We have to show honour, love, and respect to the older generation, also in the way we deal with these brothers and sisters.

I should like to summarize the whole matter as follows:

a. The Bible clearly teaches us that we have to show honour and respect to the elderly, although age is not always a guarantee of wisdom (see Job 32:6-10).

b. We should permit the elderly to remain involved in all kinds of activities as much as possible, but it can be a proof of wisdom when an elderly person gives up a position before it becomes too much for him and takes on a job which he still can handle.

c. We should leave the elderly, as much and as long as possible, in their own environment, but sometimes it is a matter of wisdom to move them to a smaller apartment in order for them to remain independent.

d. It would be wonderful if all elderly people could remain in a family setting, but sometimes placing them in a nursing home is almost inevitable.

e. Not only for widows, but for all of us, counts what the apostle Paul writes to Timothy. Let us all learn our religious duties to our family members and make some return to our parents and to the older generation in general, for that is acceptable in the sight of God (cp. I Timothy 5:3).

CHAPTER SIX

The task of a mother in a family

1. Equal rights?

We are living in the era of feminism. Everywhere we hear people talk about equal rights and equal opportunities. The classic role of a woman — taking care of her household and raising children — has to be abandoned. A woman should have the same rights as a man. It is discriminatory to deny a married woman the opportunity to have a job and to take part in social life in the same way as her husband. The burden of raising children should be shared in an equitable way. It is already a thorn in the flesh of some feminists that only a woman can bear the burden of being pregnant. However, that is a "natural phenomenon" which no one can change. (If they could, they certainly would.) The inequality should not be made worse by forcing a different role upon a woman and denying her equal rights with a man.

That is the modern philosophy. We can find it in the feminist movement as well as in the government's Affirmative Action Program. We can see the spin-off effect in many churches: women are allowed to serve as office-bearers; in some churches only as deacons, in other churches also as elders and as ministers.

It is becoming a rare phenomenon that a mother stays home all day to run the household. Many consider it degrading for a woman to be confined to "dusting, cooking, and making the beds," as it is sometimes called denigratingly. That is a dull, boring job. Intelligent women in this era of feminism deserve better.

How are we as Christians supposed to react, and what should our attitude be towards all this? In what follows I will pay attention to a number of aspects which might too often be overlooked.

As is the case with many movements, also in this one there is an element of truth in some of the complaints. The task of a mother is sometimes underestimated and undervalued. A job in an office or a professional career is often considered to be more important, to give more satisfaction, and to be more exciting than that of a housewife. However, going to the extreme causes people to fall into the very fault which they say they are fighting or correcting.

Many married women have a job, and want to keep their job for a number of years before they have children. Others keep their job even though they have children and send their children to a day care center, or the children have to manage without the parents for a couple of hours when they come home from school.

The basic reason for this development is not that being a housewife is an unimportant, boring job, or that such a role is imposed upon a married woman in a discriminatory manner. The underlying cause is that people underestimate the importance of the task of a housewife, and that they do not have enough respect for this position. This lack of respect on the part of the feminists is truly discriminatory.

Before we turn to the Biblical guidelines on this matter, we will pay attention to some other points which play an important role today. One of them is the Affirmative Action Program of the federal government.

2. Affirmative Actions

In chapter VIII objections are made to the work of labour unions and concerns are expressed about the way they deal with certain issues. However, credit should be given when credit is due. The CLAC (Christian Labour Association of Canada) has made a submission to the federal government as a warning signal against the Affirmative Action Program. The submission, entitled *"Affirmative Actions: The Perils of Social Engineering,"* is certainly worth studying by all who are interested in this matter. A firm stand is taken against the undermining of family life. Because this brochure has been sent to all church ministers to be used as resource material, I will use it as such in what follows.

The intention of the federal government's Affirmative Action Program is to make equality in employment mandatory in the public sector and to put strong pressure on the private sector to do the same.

What does "equality in employment" mean? Part of it is "equal pay for work of equal value." That sounds reasonable. However, it is not as clear-cut a matter as it seems to be. It does not simply mean that a male and a female worker should be paid equally if they are doing the same job. That is "equal pay for equal work." But "equal pay for work of equal value" means that every job has to be classified and "valued" according to a number of criteria. The relative value of a truck driver's job, of a secretary's job, of a firefighter's job, of a nurse's job, must be determined. In this evaluation the difference between typical male and female jobs is to be eliminated.

Another aspect of this Affirmative Action Program is that an employer has to hire an equal number of male and female workers, and that the average income of male and female workers has to be the same.

However, this whole system ignores the reality of the market mechanism called *the law of supply and demand*. It also ignores the fact that male and female workers are not equal. If a certain job can be done in a better way by women, more women will be hired and seek employment in that field. The "value" of a certain job cannot be determined in an artificial way. Such a system can only be used, and it will only work, as long as it is completely enforced by law. In general, the market and the law of supply and demand will determine the "value" of a certain job. If a particular job is largely overpaid, more applicants will be attracted, the "supply" will increase, and the "value" will go down. On the other hand, if a job is grossly underpaid, few will apply for the job, and the law of supply and demand will increase its "value." That is why some unpleasant or dangerous jobs have comparatively high wages to attract people. The same counts for jobs for which qualifications are required which can be met by only a few. The astronomical amounts of money paid for professionals in sports is a prime example.

Another case in point is a mandatory minimum wage for young employees. If, by legislation, this minimum wage is set too high, increased unemployment will result among young workers, because most employers will prefer an experienced worker to an apprentice or another young worker who has to be paid a relatively high wage.

It is an undeniable fact that the government has the duty to intervene when certain groups or individuals fall victim to an abuse of power or circumstances, or of unwarranted profit-making at the cost of people who are in a defenceless position. However, the whole idea behind the Affirmative Action Program is based on a wrong concept. Men and women are not equal. Both have their unique characteristics. The Affirmative Action Program flees from reality. In professional sports this idea will never be accepted. It simply is not realistic. In the Olympics, as well as in professional sports, males are not allowed to compete against females, and visa versa, in running, jumping, swimming or any other branch of sports, and no one complains about discrimination or asks for affirmative action. Although one particular person might be able to beat another individual, in general men and women are not equal. That is not a matter of higher or lower, of more or less "value." It is a matter of being different. The same applies to a job. Although in many jobs men as well as women can be hired, the fact remains that in some areas men have a natural advantage, while in other professions women, in general, are better qualified.

One of the reasons that in many "high ranking" positions less women can be found is that a great number of women with excellent qualifications do not want such a job and are not available for it. They prefer to be a mother rather than a business manager. That is also the reason why the average income of women in the workplace will be less. A great number of them leave the workforce before they have climbed the ladder to the highest possible rank. The whole concept of the Affirmative Action Program does not fight discrimination; it introduces discrimination by downplaying and undervaluating the position of a full-time housewife. Her task is considered to be less important than the task of an office worker or a business manager, while in fact her task is one of the most important and highest ranking positions available for a woman. The work of a housewife is certainly not of less value: it is invaluable, as we will see in Section 4.

Before we come to that point we will pay attention to another aspect which is mentioned quite often: the financial necessity for married women to work.

3. Financial necessity

We often hear the argument that having a job is a financial necessity for some married women. Without the mother's job, the family cannot make ends meet. This is an important point and we should not disregard it. There certainly can be a family situation where the husband, for whatever reason, cannot provide the necessary means to sustain his family. Especially when a handicap or some other health reason puts the father in a less favourable position, we should not think too lightly about the problems and the financial consequences. However, a few things have to be added to avoid a lopsided picture of the matter at stake.

I am not qualified to give advice with respect to the management of a family budget, but I am convinced that a housewife who makes a full-time job of caring for her family can save a lot of money by providing homemade things, while a mother with a job outside the house has to spend extra money for the household because she does not have the time to prepare everything herself. I agree with much of the advice given by an expert in this field, Mrs. F. VanderBoom, in her column "Around the kitchen table" in the magazine *Reformed Perspective*. I wonder whether a mother can "make" more money or save more money by staying home and making all kinds of things herself than by having a job and relying on others.

Sometimes the argument we hear is that the mother has to take on a job to earn the money necessary for sending the children to a Christian school. I will be the last one to deny the importance of a Christian education. The parents made the promise on the day their child was baptized that they would instruct the child and have him instructed according to the Word of God. But we have to keep in mind that the school cannot replace the education at home. It is extremely important for a child, when it comes home from school, to find a home where it can relax, be cared for, and find support. The child might want to talk about his problems, he may have questions which need to be dealt with. Slowly the child grows to maturity. The way guidance is given in this process of growing up can determine the course of his whole life. Recently, a specialist in the field of child raising made the remark that children today are pushed to maturity like beef cattle or chickens. There is no time for them to be children. They have to be independent and on their own too early. And, when they go in the wrong direction because of their lack of experience, the parents complain about the unmanageable youth. However, the cause is a lack of support and guidance during the process of growing to maturity. Children have to learn from someone. They need support and guidance. If the parents are too busy to give them the attention they need, they will turn to their peers, or they will be educated "in the street" or in the day care center. No one should be surprised to find that this "education" is not in line with a Christian lifestyle.

What holds true for a mother who has a job outside the house also holds true for the father who has to go out every evening. It is certainly important that a father uses his talents to serve the church and to pay home visits as an elder. But it has an adverse effect, and it is certainly wrong, when a father is so busy with all kinds of church activities that his own children do not receive enough attention. Once I overheard a boy say, "My father is so busy helping other members of the church solve their problems that he has no time to listen to me."

We should try to set the priorities straight. If a mother takes on a job to pay the school fees, and the result is that the child is on his own for some time after school, the positive effect of a Christian education may very well be surpassed by the negative effects of hanging around without proper help and support. The child should not be pushed to maturity. He should be given time to be a child and to grow up as a child, with the necessary help of parents. It certainly does not mean that the child should be sent to a public school instead, but it means that the parents must carefully consider what their priorities are. It might be necessary to cut down on other expenses. It is also possible that, by staying at home with the children, the mother can save money in the way frequently suggested by Mrs. F. VanderBoom in *Reformed Perspective.*

Another reason for taking on a job is that people can pay off their house. Not long ago someone said, "We cannot have children the first couple of years. We have to pay off our house. If we have children right away, we will not be able to send them to a Christian school." After what I have written so far, I do not need to say much about this approach. It separates what God has joined together. It is a set of wrong priorities. The one says, "We cannot afford to have children because we have to pay off a house." The other says, "We cannot afford to buy or pay off a house, because we have to raise a family." It's a matter of priorities.

4. A preeminent position

We will now pay attention to the main point of this whole discussion: the position of a housewife and the importance of her task. What does the Bible say about it? Is the task of a housewife a dull, boring, and unimportant job? Is she just confined to what is denigratingly called "dusting, cooking, and making the beds?" The Bible speaks in a completely different way in Proverbs 31:10-31.

The position of a housewife is not an unimportant one, but one of the most eminent positions in life. Today there are discussions about the question whether a woman can be an office-bearer in the church, but many neglect or downplay the most important office a woman can have in life. Proverbs 31:10 says that it is difficult to find someone who qualifies for this office. "A good wife who can find?" Is the task of a housewife unimportant? Proverbs 31:10 says that a housewife "is far more precious than jewels."

People consider the role of a housewife dull and boring. A woman has the right to take on a more important, more rewarding, and more exciting job. However, in Proverbs 31:10-27 we read:

A good wife who can find?
She is far more precious than jewels.
The heart of her husband trusts in her,
    and he will have no lack of gain.
She does him good, and no harm, all the days of her life.
She seeks wool and flax, and works with willing hands.
She is like the ships of the merchant,
    she brings her food from afar.
She rises while it is yet night and provides food for her
    household and tasks for her maidens.
She considers a field and buys it;
    with the fruits of her hands she plants a vineyard.
She girds her loins with strength
    and makes her arms strong.
She perceives that her merchandise is profitable.
Her lamp does not go out at night.
She puts her hands to the distaff,
    and her hands hold the spindle.
She opens her hand to the poor,
    and reaches out her hands to the needy.
She is not afraid of snow for her household,
    for all her household are clothed in scarlet.
She makes herself coverings;
    her clothing is fine linen and purple.
Her husband is known in the gates,
    when he sits among the elders of the land.
She makes linen garments and sells them;
    she delivers girdles to the merchant.
Strength and dignity are her clothing,
    and she laughs at the time to come.
She opens her mouth with wisdom,
    and the teaching of kindness is on her tongue.
She looks well to the ways of her household,
    and does not eat the bread of idleness.

This is one great eulogy on the preeminent position of the housewife. That is certainly not the picture of a dull job. On the contrary, it is a very exciting position. She rises early in the morning. She looks like someone who is running an important business. She provides food and makes clothing. She even buys and sells merchandise. Apparently she also knits and weaves clothes for others. That is the way she makes money and runs her business.

We find the conclusion of this "resume" or *curriculum vitae* in verses 28-31.

Her children rise up and call her blessed;
    her husband also, and he praises her:
"Many women have done excellently,
    but you surpass them all."

Charm is deceitful, and beauty is vain,
  but a woman who fears the LORD is to be praised.
Give her of the fruit of her hands,
  and let her works praise her in the gates.

Here the housewife is praised. How often does that really happen? The greatest discrimination today is that people do not value this position in the Biblical way. In excellence she surpasses many. It is a preeminent role. Let us not adapt to the worldly standards and the theory of feminists, which is destroying the most excellent role and preeminent position of a housewife.

We do not need women in office in the consistories. But they are certainly not less important. No glamour of a professional job can compete with the excellence described in Proverbs 31. That is the most desirable and rewarding office for a woman. That is one of the most important offices in the Christian church. Let us not ignore this Biblical teaching.

5. Continuous education

We already mentioned that the effect of an education in a Christian school can be surpassed by the bad effects of a lack of parental support. We have to keep in mind that education is a perpetual process. An unceasing, ongoing education takes place. Although parents and children are not always aware of it, it is tremendously important that children receive continual and consistent guidance. The way in which they are guided and supported by the mother before they go to kindergarten and after they come home from school, can determine their future. It is all the little things they hear, the questions they ask, the answers they get, and the atmosphere they live in that prepare them for their future. It is not how much academic knowledge they gather, but whether they are taught the right way of life that is determinative.

In our Western world many children are left on their own, forced and pushed to maturity. They grow up in the street or are sent to a day care center. Specialists in the field of child rearing are concerned about the increasing frustration among children. Many are unhappy and dissatisfied in spite of the luxury in which they live. Many are desperate and seek refuge in drugs or commit suicide. In the Soviet Union they seem to be more aware of the importance of child rearing. Many children there are trained and raised in government-ruled institutions. They are systematically, and very strictly, indoctrinated already at a very young age. And it works. While we should not adopt their system, it shows us how important early childhood is, and what consistent and unceasing education can bring about.

God has created the family as a haven of security for children, where they can grow up with the necessary support and guidance from their parents. Among the people of Israel great emphasis was, and still is, put on family life. The children were educated in the first place within the family. The father and the mother had the most important place in this process. In Proverbs 1:8,9 we read, "Hear, my son, your father's instruction, and reject not your mother's teaching; for they are a fair garland for your head, and pendants for your neck." Let us keep in honour this Biblical pattern. Not what the feminist movement tries to make us believe should determine our opinion, but what Holy Scripture says about the preeminent office of a housewife "more precious than jewels."

6. Who pays the bill?

Let us be on the alert to set our priorities straight. We have seen and heard of parents who work hard to make as much money as possible. The father virtually works day and night and has no time to talk with his children. The mother has a job and the children have to look after themselves when they come home from school, or they are brought to a day care center. The parents can afford all kinds of luxury. The children are spoiled with too much pocket money and expensive toys. However, the tragic result is that after a number of years, when the house is paid off, the children are gone. They have found other places to go to. When the parents finally have the time and the desire to talk with their children, it is too late: the children have no line of communication with their parents.

This is certainly not the general picture. Fortunately not. It is somewhat overstated to emphasize the danger. But many parents may recognize some aspects of their own situation in it. I hope that it gives food for thought to keep us on the right track. It is easy to complain about youngsters who get into mischief or who are unmanageable. Parents can try hard to correct a rebellious boy when he is fourteen years old, but it is much better and more effective to begin fourteen years earlier, being involved with the ongoing education of the child. It might be nice or even necessary to a certain extent to provide some extra income for the family. However, if it is done at the cost of attention for the children while they are young, the parents sometimes have to pay dearly for it later. They may have to pay the bill in a way they had never expected.

Therefore, let us not underestimate the importance of the task of a housewife. She is a woman in the most feminine office, more precious than jewels.

The relationship between employer and employee

1. Traditionalism

In this chapter I will discuss some aspects of the relationship between employer and employee. I will pay attention to the value of labour according to Biblical notions, the relationship between labour and capital in the modern production process, the relationship between labour and ownership, the responsibility of the labourers for and their involvement in the fruits of their labour, and some related issues. I will also trace how the Bible speaks about possession, ownership, wealth, riches and stewardship. A closely related matter is the question of authority and obedience in labour relations; where does the authority and the right of the employer end and what is the extent and what are the limitations of the required obedience of the employee?

These matters are being discussed today. We can hear all kinds of revolutionary ideas. But we must be careful that we do not stick to old traditions because they are old. People have tried to defend the employment of slaves on Biblical grounds. Most Christians today agree that slavery is not an acceptable system, although it is a very old tradition, even mentioned as having existed to a certain extent in the time of the early Christian churches.

There is a danger in the modern movement for "human" and "equal" rights. Quite often there is a revolutionary concept behind it: a system that tries to get rid of all Biblical notions of authority and obedience. All moral norms are rejected. Man becomes his own norm, and everyone has to decide for himself. Few people care about the commandments of the Lord regarding labour relations.

In this confusing development, specifically with respect to labour relations, we will search the Word of God to see and hear what the Bible teaches us.

2. Ownership and labour

When we discuss labour relations and the value of labour according to Biblical notions, we first have to consider the relationship between labour and capital, those being two of the main factors in the production process. We can also call it the relationship between the labourer and the owner of the company or between labour and investment.

The production system in our country is sometimes called a capitalistic system as opposed to the communistic system. We can also call it free enterprise versus the socialistic system.

There is a lot of confusion about these terms. What, exactly do we mean by them? For a fruitful discussion, it is always important first to define the terms, in order to make clear what we have in mind when we use them.

The basic difference between the systems, as far as our topic is concerned, is the question whether the production system is a matter of private ownership or national ownership, and whether it is a system of free enterprise, ruled by the laws of supply and demand, or a system completely ruled by the government.

What is the meaning of the capital or investment factor in the production process?

According to Webster's dictionary, capital means: "Any form of wealth employed for the production of more wealth; the wealth thus employed by a business or industrial or commercial enterprise, which can be in the form of manufactured goods, money, stocks or bonds, or relatively permanent assets as machinery or buildings."

The three main factors in the production process are labour, resources and capital. It is clear that capital is an important factor in this respect. It has to do with wealth and the production of wealth. Although the Bible does not use the word "capital" as such, the matter is dealt with in many instances. The Bible speaks in various places about wealth and the "production of wealth," about the possession of goods and the increase of someone's possessions.

3. Holy Scripture on wealth and ownership

Possession of goods, ownership and wealth are mentioned quite often in the Bible and certainly not in a negative way. The Bible does not condemn riches and wealth. On the contrary. We read in Genesis 13:2 that Abraham was very rich in cattle, in silver and in gold. We even read that the LORD had made him rich.

According to chapter 1:3, Job was the greatest or richests of the people of the east. There was nothing wrong with that. He was tested by the LORD and tempted by the devil — not because he was rich, but to show the victory of God's mercy and grace in his life. After he stood the test, the LORD gave him back all his possessions — yes, even twice as much as he had in the beginning.

In the Acts of the Apostles we read about people, members of the church, who were owners of land and other possessions. Some sold their possessions to give the proceeds to the poor. Ananias and Sapphira were punished, not because they had personal possessions or because they did not give all their money to the poor. They were punished because they lied and pretended something which was not true. The apostle Peter says in chapter 5:4 "While it remained unsold, did it not remain your own? And after it was sold, was it not at your disposal? How is it that you have contrived this deed in your heart? You have not lied to men but to God." Their sin was not that they kept their own possessions for themselves, but that they "tempted the Spirit of the Lord" (Acts 5:9).

In Matthew 19:21 we read about a rich young man who came to Jesus and wanted to follow the Lord. Finally he left Jesus, because he was unable to give up his possessions. His fault was not that he was rich and that he had many possessions. He failed because he trusted in his possessions and would sooner give up Christ than his wealth. He did not possess his wealth but his wealth had taken possession of him.

The Bible teaches us that wealth and riches can be a blessing from the Lord, just as it was with Abraham, with Job and with Solomon. But we are also taught that it can be a danger. Those who are rich are in danger of being led astray by their possessions and of being captured by their wealth. The Bible warns us about amassing many possessions without being rich in the Lord.

Riches and wealth must be governed by good stewardship.

4. The Bible on stewardship

We have to be good and responsible stewards of the things the Lord has entrusted to us.

The word "steward" has more than one meaning in our language and is used in different ways. Therefore it is important to notice the Biblical meaning. A steward, in the Bible, is not just a servant, as in a restaurant or in an airplane. Neither is he just a bookkeeper who looks after the business, as we see with some landlords today.

A steward, in Biblical times, was a very important person, who was completely in charge of all the possessions of his master. He acted on behalf of his master and ran his whole business. He had almost unlimited power, and his master entrusted all his possessions to him, especially during his absence.

In Genesis 39:4 we read about Joseph in the house of Potiphar. He was a steward in the house of his master. He is called "an overseer of his house, in charge of all that he had." In chapter 39:6 Joseph says that his master left all that he had in Joseph's hand, having no concern for anything but the food which he ate. That is why Joseph said to Potiphar's wife in chapter 39:9, "He has not left back anything from me except yourself, because you are his wife."

That shows us the important position of a steward. The Lord has made us stewards. He has entrusted to us His possessions. All our wealth, all our possessions are His. Whether there are many or few, we will be called to account for the way we have used and put to use our possessions.

That places a great responsibility on those who are blessed with wealth and many possessions.

5. Acquiring possessions

How do we acquire possessions? Basically there are two different ways: either through our own labour or by receiving gifts. We can acquire possessions as a reward for our efforts or as a heritage. One grows rich as a fruit of his own labour while another becomes rich because of his parent's wealth. Both are mentioned in the Bible.

In the Old Testament we often read about the latter: possessions received without any effort, just as a gift. About Abraham we read that the LORD had made him rich and had given him everything. He did not even accept a gift from the King of Sodom, lest the king should say, "I have made Abram rich" (Genesis 14:20-15:1). The LORD made Abraham rich. He received the land and all other things as an inheritance out of the hand of the LORD.

Also Job received back all his wealth out of the hand of the LORD, yes even twice as much as he had in the beginning.

The Bible quite often speaks about obtaining possessions without any effort, as a gift or an inheritance — sometimes directly out of His hand, sometimes as an inheritance from the parents. That is a legitimate way of obtaining possessions. Although today there is a tendency to condemn the acquisition of possessions without personal effort, the Bible speaks differently about it. The most important point is not how we obtain our possessions, but whether we take care of them in a responsible manner, as stewards over what the Lord has entrusted to us.

The Bible speaks not only about ownership by inheritance, but also about obtaining possessions as a result of labour. That brings us to our next point.

6. Scriptural notions of labour

If we wish to investigate the relationship between labour and capital, we must first pay attention to what the Bible says about labour.

Nowadays labour is considered one of the three main factors in the production process. These three factors are: labour, capital and resources. In some types of industry capital is more important, in others labour is the main factor, while still others depend almost completely on the availability of natural resources. However, in most types of industry all three components are necessary. In our present economic situation labour is seen as a separate factor. It is something you can sell. It is a commodity and the price depends on the mechanism of supply and demand. Unemployment brings down the "price" of labour and overemployment tends to cause the price to increase. You have to pay more for high-quality labour or for a skill that has become rare. Employers and manufacturers try to get labour for the lowest possible price. A labour contract is considered to be of the same nature as a contract for the delivery of some pieces of equipment. It is the result of hard bargaining. That dehumanizes human labour and reduces it to a "product" that can be bought or sold.

The Bible speaks about labour in a different way. It is remarkable that in the Bible labour is closely associated with the fruits of labour. In the original language of the Old Testament different words are used which are and can be translated by *labour*. Some are used only once or a few times and are of less importance for our topic. Some words pay special attention to the activity of the worker: being busy with something. Others emphasize the creation of something: making or developing a product.

There are two words that are of great importance for our understanding of this matter. The one stresses the difficulty, trouble and pain of labour, while the other puts all emphasis on the results or the fruits of one's labour.

Starting with the first one, we will look at a few texts. For clarity's sake and just so you are not bothered with Hebrew words, we will compare the King James Version (KJV) with the Revised Standars version (RSV).

In Deuteronomy 26:7 we read about the people of Israel in Egypt. They said (according to the KJV): "The LORD heard our voice, and looked at our affliction, and our *labour*, and our oppression." In the RSV we read: "The LORD heard our voice, and saw our affliction, our *toil*, and our oppression." The word *labour* in the KJV is replaced by *toil*, in the RSV as well as in the New American Standard Bible (NASB) and in the New International Version (NIV).

We find the same in Ecclesiastes 4:9 (and in many other texts in the book of Ecclesiastes): "Two are better than one; because they have a good reward for their *labour*" (KJV). The RSV renders this by ". . . they have a good reward for their *toil*."

From these two texts we can learn that a word is used that can be translated by *labour*, but that emphasizes the struggle, pain and trouble of labour. The same word is translated in other texts by *travail*, *anguish* or *suffering*. That is one aspect of labour. Through sin labour has become a burden, a toil, and a pain. The same meaning of this word is used when a mother is about to give birth to a baby: we say she is "in labour."

This shows us one important aspect of our daily work and effort. Sin has infected our entire life. Since Genesis 3:17-19 our labour lies under the curse of the LORD. The LORD said to Adam: "Because you have listened to the voice of your wife, and have eaten of the tree of which I commanded you, 'You shall not eat of it,' cursed is the ground because of you; in toil you shall eat of it all the days of your life; thorns and thistles it shall bring forth to you; and you shall eat the plants of the field. In the sweat of your face you shall eat bread till you return to the ground, for out of it you are taken; you are dust, and to dust you shall return."

7. The fruits of our labour

There is another word used in the Old Testament, however, that is translated by the word *labour*. That word indicates more specifically the results and the fruits of labour.

In Ezekiel 23:29 the punishment of the LORD is pronounced on Israel. The LORD will give them into the hand of their enemies. "They shall deal with thee hatefully, and shall take away all thy *labour*" (KJV). The RSV says: "They shall deal with you in hatred, and take away all *the fruits of your labour*." Here, apparently, *labour* can also be translated by *fruits of labour*.

In Isaiah 45:14 we read in the KJV that the LORD will give into the hand of His people Israel "the *labour* of Egypt." The RSV speaks about "the *wealth* of Egypt."

We find another example in Hosea 12:8. The KJV has: "In all my *labours* they shall find none iniquity in me that were sin." The NIV renders this as "With all my *wealth* they will not find in me any iniquity or sin." The RSV speaks here about *riches*. So labour is translated by *wealth* and *riches*.

To mention just one more, we will look at Isaiah 55:2. In this well-known text we read in the KJV: "Wherefore do you spend money for that which is not bread? and your *labour* for that which satisfieth not?" In the NASB we read: "Why do you spend money for what is not bread, and your *wages* for what does not satisfy?" Here we find *labour* translated by *wages*.

We are not going to discuss which translation is better or more to the point. What I have tried to make clear is that one and the same word, translated in the KJV by *labour*, can be rendered also as *riches*, *wealth*, *wages* and *fruits of labour*.

This shows us the flavour of this word. It also makes clear that the Biblical notion of labour is closely associated with the results of labour. Labour is not just something you can buy and sell for the most reasonable price. Labour is inseparably connected with its fruits.

This connection shows the responsibility of the labourer for the result of his work. It also shows the relationship between labour and the profits made by it. The fruits of labour are part of labour and of the labourer. The word *labour* can even be translated in some cases by *wealth*, *riches* and *wages*. That is what we have to keep in mind when we discuss the involvement of the labourers in the results and the profits of the company.

Nowadays we hear about all kinds of revolutionary actions. There are labourers who occupy a plant and take over a company. There are those who close down a business by a strike, and there are those who try to keep operating a company which is to be closed by its owners.

We have to be careful in our judgment. Although we have to call a spade a spade and condemn all illegal actions and any revolutionary approach, we have to be aware of the Biblical notion of labour and the close relationship between labour on the one hand, and the fruits of the labour, the wealth and the riches derived from it, on the other hand.

Every owner has to be a steward who acts responsibly. The Lord has set him over the possessions entrusted to him. He is not free to do with his business what he likes to do. He must give account of all his doings to the Lord. He has to show his responsibility. "His" wealth might very well be, to a certain extent, the fruit of the labour of his employees. Therefore, according to the Biblical notion of labour, he has a responsibility towards his employees. Mismanagement on his part makes him guilty; it makes him a bad steward in the sight of the Lord, causing him also to fall short in his responsibility towards his employees.

Today we hear about getting workers involved in management decisions. While that can be a revolutionary development, it can also be a sound and Biblical move. Take, for instance, a situation in which certain people have worked almost their whole life in a certain factory and have given all they had to build up the company. It is not fair for the management then, all of a sudden, to decide to move the plant to another area in the country, because there they can pay lower wages. The management is not just dealing with "its" own company, but with a part of the life of the employees. It can be a matter of good stewardship to discuss such a move with the labourers involved, and to consider their interests as well. The same counts when a manufacturer decides to buy some parts in another country, instead of making them in his own plant. If that means a massive lay-off of people who have worked in the business for many years, then the company has to consider that the factory is, to a certain extent, also the fruit of the labour of their workers, and part of their life. They cannot just lay them off like a piece of equipment. The Bible clearly shows us the close relationship between labour on the one hand, and the fruits of the labour, the riches, the wealth and the possession derived from it, on the other hand.

That can have far-reaching consequences, as we will see in what follows.

8. Ownership and authority

We are living in an anarchistic world. *Anarchy* means the absence of order, discipline and authority. It is a situation of lawlessness, and of social and political disorder, caused by a lack of respect for the government and for all those who are in authority.

Authority and obedience seem to be old-fashioned matters. Everyone talks about rights, about constitutional rights and human rights, but few seem concerned about obligations. There is a tendency in our society to take sides with criminals rather than with police officers who have to fight against crime. Murderers and other criminals are protected, their constitutional rights are defended, sometimes even in an absurd manner — all at the cost of the victims of their crimes.

We see the same tendency in social life. Ownership is almost considered a dirty word. Authority and obedience are wornout notions. The labourers, or rather, the big bosses of the labour unions, dictate their rules, and the company owner simply has to obey; otherwise his business will be closed down by a strike and he will be driven into bankruptcy. That is what they call "hard bargaining." In such a situation it is important to listen to the Word of God, to find out what our attitude should be in this respect.

First we will pay attention to what the Bible says about the master-slave relationship. Next we will see in how far and in what way we can apply this to labour relations today.

9. The relationship between master and slave

The Bible often speaks about the relationship between master and slave. Before we apply this to labour relations today, we should first consider what the nature of such a relationship was.

In Ephesians 6:5 we read "Slaves, be obedient to those who are your earthly masters, with fear and trembling, in singleness of heart, as to Christ."

We find almost the same in Colossians 3:22: "Slaves, obey in everything those who are your earthly masters, not with eyeservice, as men-pleasers, but in singleness of heart, fearing the Lord."

The apostle Paul writes in his letter to Titus, chapter 2:9: "Bid slaves to be submissive to their masters and to give satisfaction in every respect; they are not to be refractory."

The apostle Peter writes in chapter 2:18 of his first letter: "Servants, be submissive to your masters with all respect, not only to the kind and gentle but also to the overbearing."

That is clear language. We can also mention Romans 13:1: "Let every person be subject to the governing authorities. For there is no authority except from God, and those that exist have been instituted by God."

The Bible speaks about obedience and submissiveness. We have to obey not only the gentle, but also the overbearing, masters. The apostle speaks about obedience without gainsaying or backtalk.

When we read all this, we may wonder whether we can apply this to labour relations today.

Sometimes these texts have been used to defend slavery as a system. Is that correct? No, it is not. We have to consider the circumstances in which the apostles were speaking. They did not live in the same situation as we today, neither did they live in a situation of slavery like the one that existed about one century ago in the United States.

We have to realize, in the first place, that the mentioning of slavery in the Bible, and the instructions of the apostles given to the slaves, do not condone the system of slavery. An example can make clear what I mean by this. An airline company gives instruction to its crew on how to deal with hijackers. Generally speaking, they are to give in to their demands, to avoid a confrontation and the killing of people. That does not mean that the airline company in any way condones the actions of or sympathize with the hijackers. Not at all. They simply give instructions on how to deal with specific problems in an certain situation, to show the crew how they can prevent fatalities, not to justify the actions of the hijackers.

To a certain extent it is the same when the apostle gives instruction to the slaves on how to act when they have overbearing masters. They must be obedient. That does not justify the attitude of the masters: it simply tells Christian slaves how they have to live.

That is one point we have to consider, but there is more. The apostle also gives instruction to the masters. In Ephesians 6:9 we read: "Masters, do the same to them that is, be aware of your responsibility to the Lord, and forbear threatening, knowing that He who is both their Master and yours is in heaven, and that there is no partiality with Him." And in Colossians 4:1 we read: "Masters, treat your slaves justly and fairly, knowing that you also have a Master in heaven." Apparently there were masters who dealt with their slaves justly and fairly, in a Christian way, as brothers in the Lord.

Apart from this we have to keep in mind that the position of the slaves in Israel, especially in the time of the Old Testament, but also in the time of the apostles, was quite different from the position of slaves in this part of the world at the end of the nineteenth and the beginning of the twentieth century.

Let us first pay some attention to the positions of slaves in the Old Testament.

10. Slaves in the Old Testament

The slaves of Abraham's day were not just rightless people who were bought and sold without any concern for human dignity. On the contrary. They had certain rights and privileges. They belonged to the household of the master and could count on his protection. They even shared in the promises of the covenant as members of the family. In Genesis 17:13 we read: "Both he that is born in your house and he that is bought with your money, shall be circumcised. So shall My covenant be in your flesh an everlasting covenant." That is quite something. The slaves were considered to be members of the family and shared in the promises of the LORD as members of the church, incorporated in the covenant of the LORD.

They also had legal rights with respect to the possessions of their master. In our country, according to the law, one's legal heirs are, in the first place, one's children, and, if there are no children, then one's brothers and sisters, one's parents (if they are still alive), or one's nephews and nieces. Employees will never become heirs, unless so specified in one's last will and testament.

That was different in Abraham's time. In Genesis 15:2-4 we read: "But Abram said, 'O LORD God, what wilt Thou give me, for I continue childless, and the heir of my house is Eliezer of Damascus?' And Abram said, 'Behold, Thou hast given me no offspring; and a slave born in my house will be my heir.' And behold, the word of God came to him, 'This man shall not be your heir; your own son shall be your heir.' " Abram did not have children as yet. Apparently, in that situation "the heir of his house" was Eliezer of Damascus, a slave born in his house. As far as the rights of heirs were concerned, this slave came before Abram's own brothers Nahor and Haran and before his nephew Lot.

That makes perfectly clear that we cannot compare the position of slaves in Abram's time with the position of the slaves in the United States about a century ago. Nor can we compare the position of these slaves with the employees in a company nowadays. Slaves belonged to the family of their master and to the spiritual community as members of the church, circumcised as heirs of the covenant.

To understand the relationship of authority and obedience, we must elaborate on the structure of the government at that time.

11. Patriarchal government

The word *patriarchal* literally means: ruled and governed by the father, the head of the family.

70

In our present social and political situation we can make a distinction between the authority of parents, the authority of office-bearers in the church, and the authority of civil governments. They all have their own responsibility, their own jusrisdiction, and their own task. Although their authority is not contradictory, it is still quite different. The fifth commandment says: Honour your father and your mother. That is the first time we are confronted with the authority given by the LORD in human life. Children have to obey their parents, because it pleases the LORD to govern them by their hand. Lord's Day 39 broadens the meaning of this commandment and says that we have to show honour, love and faithfulness to all those in authority over us. It is clear that we have to include in this the authority of office-bearers in the church and the authority of the civil governments. They all are set over us by the Lord and it pleases Him to govern us by their hand.

However, in the time of the Old Testament the situation was different. There was no distinction between the task of parents and that of office-bearers in the church and that of civil governments. In the patriarchal system the head of the family, the "father" or patriarch, was at the same time the religious and political head of the community. We still find this system among the Bedouins in the modern State of Israel today. In judicial matters, a patriarch had about the same jurisdiction as a mayor and a Justice of the Peace together have in our country. He was both the political and the religious leader of the community. A "family" consisted of a group of people. It included not just the parents and their little children, but also the married children and their children. It constituted a sort of "tribe."

When we read in the Old Testament about slaves, we have to keep in mind that they lived in such a patriarchal system. Their master was not only their employer; he was also the head of the family and the political and religious leader. Today we make a distinction between the authority of parents, of office-bearers in the church, and of civil governments. We recognize them, each in their own place, as having been set in authority over us. In the Old Testament it was one and the same person who was in charge of all these duties.

When we read in the Bible about the obedience and submissiveness required of slaves to their masters, we must realize that it was an obedience at the same level as our obedience on our parents, the office-bearers, and the civil government. It was the relationship referred to in the fifth commandment.

A slave was not just a servant without any rights. He was a member of the family, with certain specific rights, even rights concerning inheritance. He was a member of the church, circumcised on the eighth day. He was under the legal jurisdiction of his master and had to serve him, even in the army, as we can learn from Genesis 14:14. That is why we cannot simply apply to our present labour relations all what is said in the Bible about slaves.

Now you might say: "That is all fine and dandy, but the apostle spoke in a different situation. Not all masters in his time treated their slaves in the way Abraham did." That is right. And that is why the apostle Paul writes in Ephesians 6:9, "Masters, do the same to them that is, as servants of Christ, doing the will of God from the heart, and forbear threatening, knowing that He who is both their Master and yours is in heaven, and that there is no partiality with Him." And in Colossians 4:1 he writes: "Masters, treat your slaves justly and fairly, knowing that you also have a Master in heaven." Apparently, not all masters acted the way they were supposed to. The apostle warns them to be aware of their responsibility.

From the foregoing we can draw the following conclusions:

a. the position of the slaves in the Old testament was completely different from the present relationship between employer and employee;

b. the apostle admonishes slaves, who have to suffer because of overbearing masters not to act in a revolutionary way;

c. the apostle does not condone such wrong situations, but he admonishes also the masters to act justly and fairly toward their slaves.

In the time of the apostles there was undoubtedly already a change in the social pattern, especially in the relationship between master and slave, but it is clear from what we have seen so far that we cannot equate the situation in that time with the present labour relations situation.

To be able to deal properly with the implications of this matter, I first have to say more about various aspects of authority, power and leadership.

12. Authority, power, and leadership

Among modern sociologists there is a discussion going on about the meaning of, and the difference between, power and authority. To have power means that someone is in a position to force others to act the way he prefers, or that he can use his influence to change the course of events according to his desires. To have authority, according to some sociologists, means that one has moral supremacy and is accepted in his position by his environment, by his colleagues or by his subjects. A well-known sociologist stated that authority means: accepted leadership.

The former needs no further explanation. A position of power means that someone can force others to submission and obedience, whether he has the legal right or not. A hijacker and a terrorist have power; they can force people, in fear of their lives, to do anything they wish.

However, the latter can have far-reaching and unforeseen social consequences. If we define authority as an accepted position of leadership, the matter of authority becomes questionable and depends on the attitude of the public and its acceptance by the subjects. A police officer can use power, but he has authority only when his position is accepted by the people. A teacher can have a powerful position, but his authority depends on whether he is accepted by the students. Parents can punish their children, but they have to show their authority by ensuring that their position is accepted. According to this theory, the legality and legitimacy of someone's position depends on the reaction of the public or the subjects.

It is certainly important for someone who has authority and who is in a high position to make sure that his policy and his decisions are accepted by his subjects. We can even call it a matter of moral authority that a teacher develops a good relationship with his students and that he manages to make his students accept his decisions. Parents who yell at their children all the time without any results, are not doing a good job. It is really important for someone in authority to see that he is accepted by his subjects. However, that does not take away his legal right. Even though students cannot get along with their teacher or children do not agree with their parents, they still have to be obedient. Their disagreement does not give them the right to go their own way. In other words, the authority of parents, teachers and governments does not depend on *acceptance* by the people. It is a mandate given by the Lord. That is what the Bible teaches us, and that is what we can learn from Lord's Day 39 Heidelberg Catechism: We have to show all honour, love and faithfulness to all those in authority over us. We have to submit ourselves with due obedience to their good instruction, *since* it is God's will to govern us by their hand.

According to our confession the legitimacy of authority does not depend on acceptance by the subjects. We believe that authority is given by the Lord. He has set some persons in authority over us. That is why we reject the modern notion of "accepted leadership" as the definition of authority.

We must make a distinction between power and authority, but, instead of using the definition of modern sociologists, we should use the definition given by the late Prof. B. Holwerda.[1] He makes a distinction between the Biblical (Greek) words *dunamis* and *exousia*. *Dunamis* can be translated by *power*, the actual position of power, used for instance by a burglar, a gangster or a hijacker. It indicates the ability to force others to be obedient and submissive. *Exousia* indicates a mandate given by the Lord. It refers to an office, a task and responsibility to govern and rule, as for instance is the case with parents, office-bearers in the church and the civil governments.

This approach is completely different from that of modern sociology. It is a concept concurring with and derived from the Word of God.

For our purposes I should like to add a third category, and that is "leadership." For clarity's sake we will use the following definitions:

Authority is based on a mandate given by the Lord to office-bearers in the church, officers of civil governments, and parents.

Power is based on the availability of means of enforcement.

Leadership is based on mutual agreement and is subject to voluntarily accepted rules.

Concerning the first category, the Bible teaches us clearly that the Lord has given authority to parents, to office-bearers in the church, and to civil governments. Lord's Day 39 speaks, in the first place, about the authority given by the Lord to parents. Romans 13 shows us that the Lord has given authority to civil governments. Hebrews 13:17 teaches us that we have to submit to the office-bearers who are set over us, to keep watch over our souls. The Bible says that we have to submit ourselves to such authority, because it pleases the Lord to govern us by their hand. Even when we think that they are unreasonable, or when we do not agree with them, we must have patience with their weaknesses and shortcomings (Heidelberg Catechism, Lord's Day 39). There is only one exception, only one situation in which we may refuse to obey and are permitted to oppose the authority, and that is when obedience would bring us in conflict with the Word of God. If that is the case, we have to be more obedient to God than to men.

The second category, called *power*, is also clear. When we are forced to do something, it may be better to give in, even though the person in power has no legal right or authority at all. That is not a matter of obedience, but it is opportune to do so in the actual situation, at least as long as it does not bring us in conflict with the Word of God. For instance, if a robber threatens you with a gun and asks you to hand over your purse, you had better give in; otherwise he might hurt you or even kill you. If he asks you to do something that goes against the Word of God, you have to refuse. If people ask you to renounce your faith or to deny your Saviour, you have to say no, even if it would cost you your life.

When the unions call a strike, they use power to force a company to give in. When a company tries to lower the wages of its employees in a time of high unemployment, it is using power. The employees have no choice but to accept it, because they would not be able to find another job.

Quite often real authority and power go together. Governments are in a position to enforce the laws. Parents can use discipline to force their children to obey the rules. It also happens that people who have authority have no power to enforce the rules. Police officers can have all the rights in the world, but they are unable, for instance, to enforce the law during a demonstration which runs out of control. Parents are sometimes also unable to make their children obey the rules, although they have the legal right to do so.

It is clear that, according to the definitions provided above, there is a distinction between authority and power, although they can go hand in hand.

The third category which was mentioned is leadership based on mutual agreement and subject to voluntarily accepted rules. That is often the case in labour relations in our present social situation. As I said earlier, there can be a position of power on either side, but that is not characteristic of this situation. There is also a relationship of authority and obedience, but this authority is not in the first place based on a direct mandate given by the Lord, but ensues from a voluntarily established agreement.

An employee has to listen to and obey his employer, within the limitations of his labour contract. A subcontractor has to follow the instructions of the contractor or the architect who is in charge. The contractor, on his part, has to follow the instructions of his principal. All these relations of authority, obedience and submissiveness are not in the first place based on a mandate given by the Lord, but on a contract or agreement.

Some labourers do not have a real labour contract with their boss; they get paid per unit of work. A painter can be paid per square foot, a bricklayer, per thousand bricks; a truck driver, per mile; and a salesman, per product sold. It makes quite a difference in what way they are subject to the leadership of their employer or principal, but they all have the responsibility to live up to the rules of their contract. The one might have a say over the other, but all within the limitations and according to the rules of their agreement. It does not really matter whether it is a written contract, a verbal agreement, a rule based upon tradition, or a gentlemen's agreement.

That brings us to the next point, the question whether we, in such cases, have to apply the fifth commandment or the ninth commandment.

13. The fifth and the ninth commandment

In the previous section we made a distinction between authority, power and leadership. All these expressions can be used in different ways; the meaning depends on the context. To prevent confusion and misunderstanding we defined the meaning of these words for the purpose of this chapter. Let us, for clarity's sake repeat them once more.

Authority is a relationship based on a mandate given by the Lord to certain office-bearers, officers and parents.

Power is a relationship based on the availability of means of enforcement.

Leadership is a relationship based on mutual agreement and subject to voluntarily accepted rules.

I referred to what Prof. B. Holwerda wrote in this respect. The Bible uses the Greek word *exousia* for a mandate given by the Lord to rule and govern with authority on His behalf. The Greek word *dunamis* emphasizes a position of power; that is, the ability to enforce obedience and to make people do what the ruler wants.

Leadership, according to our definition, does not necessarily include a mandate given by the Lord. Neither does it mean a powerful position and the ability to enforce the rules. The main characteristic of this relationship is that it is based on a voluntarily accepted agreement.

Often these three different situations are interwoven and more than one can be present. But it is important to make this distinction, to prevent wrong conclusions.

We have seen already that the relationship between master and slave in the Old Testament belonged to the first category. It was based upon the authority of the father as the head of the family. The father was at the same time the head of the community in civil matters and therefore represented the government, according to Romans 13. He was also the religious leader in charge of "church discipline." As religious leader he had to proclaim and explain the commandments of the LORD. He had to act as a priest in his house. In the time that the service of the LORD was concentrated in the temple in Jerusalem, every father or patriarch had to act as the representative of the LORD in his own family.

Our present-day labour relations do not fit the first category, nor are they determined by the rules of the second category. Of course, there are some situations in which these relations are interwoven. For someone who is in the army or who is a public servant, his employer is at the same time the Civil government. Someone who works in his father's business is simultaneously obedient to his father and to his employer. Also the aspect of power can come into the picture. At a time of high unemployment an employer can force his employees to accept things which they would not have taken hands down under normal circumstances. The opposite also happens. When there are many vacancies, an employee can make demands which would be unacceptable in a normal situation. That is simply the law of supply and demand.

Generally speaking, however, we can say that a labour relation is based upon a voluntarily accepted agreement. The employee promises to do his job and the employer is bound to pay his wages. All kinds of regulations are made. It is clear that such a labour relation includes the obligation to obey and to follow the instructions of the employer or the supervisor. To a certain extent we can speak of a relationship of authority and obedience. However, this relationship is not based upon a mandate given by the Lord. It is an agreement, a contract. Of course, both parties have to live up to this contract. That includes obedience, but in this respect we should refer to the ninth commandment rather than to the fifth. We have to love the truth in judicial and all other dealing. We have to keep our promise. A person who does not live up to his obligations is guilty according to the ninth commandment. That counts for the employee as well as for the employer. Their relationship is governed, in the first place, by the ninth commandment.

That counts not only for the relationship between employer and employee, but also for the relationship between a contractor and a principal, between an architect and a subcontractor. They all have to show fidelity and truth.

All kinds of relations of leadership, obedience and submission, where one has a say over the other, are involved in the process of labour. "He who pays the piper calls the tune."

It is remarkable that, with respect to labour relations, many think in the first place about the fifth commandment. In every relationship where someone has a say over someone else, people tend to refer to the authority mentioned in Lord's Day 39. From the foregoing it is clear that we have to make a distinction. The authority given by the Lord and referred to in the fifth commandment is the authority the Lord gave to parents, to office-bearers in the church and to civil governments. We have to obey them because it pleases the Lord to govern us by their hand. Even if we don't like them, or do not agree with them, we have to obey them and we must have patience with their weaknesses and shortcomings. Children cannot say: "I don't like my parents. I'm going to run away and try to find other guardians." Church members cannot, for personal reasons, withdraw from the congregation and join another congregation, just because they like the office-bearers in the new congregation better. Nor do we have a choice as far as the government is concerned.

There is only one limitation, and that is when obedience would bring us in conflict with the commandments of the Lord. Then the rule prevails: you shall obey the Lord more than men. In all other situations we must submit ourselves to the authority of those who are set over us by the Lord. With labour relations it is a different matter. If someone does not like his employer or if the weaknesses or shortcomings of his employer bother him, he is free to quit his job and look for another job, at least as long as he sticks to the terms of his contract, also concerning the procedure of quitting. No one will maintain that looking for another job is in conflict with the Word of God. No one will argue that it pleases the Lord to govern us by that particular boss and that we *therefore* have to bear with his weaknesses and shortcomings, without the right to quit the job. Of course, when someone finds a job, he may see it as coming out of the hand of the Lord. God's hand and His providence is in everything. But it does not mean that there is a commandment of the Lord to stay at a job indefinitely. If someone succeeds in finding another job, he may accept this as coming out of the Lord's hand as well.

A labour relation is determined by an agreement, and the obedience and submissiveness is also limited by this contract. If an employer asks something that goes beyond or exceeds the terms of the contract, the employee is free to refuse, within reasonable limits. Let me use an example to explain what I mean by this. At the beginning of this century most people in Bergentheim, the Netherlands, were peat cutters or peat diggers (turfstekers). They all worked for the same company. At that time they began to organize a Christian school. Their employer was strongly opposed to such a school and he forbade his employees to participate in these activities and to send their children to such a school. Those who ignored his warning would be fired. That was not a matter of authority, but was a show of power: there was a lot of unemployment and his employees depended on him for their living. And yet, many ignored his threat. The local minister, the Rev. Caspar Diemer, encouraged the people to ignore their employer's warning, because the school was none of their employer's business. Nonetheless many were in a tight squeeze. They considered it to be against the fifth commandment to ignore the instruction of the boss, who was set over them by the Lord. They felt guilty when they were fired. The Rev. C. Diemer, however, made clear that the employer abused his position, his "power." A Reformed school was established and the employer had to back down. It was one of the first "labour movements" in which Reformed people were involved, and the Reformed school in Bergentheim is still called Caspar Diemer School.

By emphasizing the importance of the ninth commandment with respect to labour relations, I do not mean that the fifth commandment does not count. Sometimes people talk about it as being a matter of either the fifth or the ninth commandment, but I consider that a false dilemma, as we will see in the next section.

14. The unity of the Law

In James 2:10-11 we read: "For whoever keeps the whole law but fails in one point has become guilty of all of it. For He who said, 'Do not commit adultery,' said also, 'Do not kill.' If you do not commit adultery but do kill, you have become a transgressor of the law." The Law of the Lord is one and has to be considered as a unity. I tell my catechism students that we cannot mention any sin which is just against *one* of the commandments, and not against the other. A person who makes a false presentation on his income tax return, sins against the fifth commandment (disobedience to the government), against the eighth commandment (he steals), and against the ninth commandment (he gives false witness). When a young couple expect a baby before they are married, they have obviously sinned against the tenth commandment (not even the slightest thought or desire contrary to any of God's commandments should ever arise in your heart) and against the fifth commandment (honour your father and your mother), but we call it sin against the seventh commandment, because that is considered the most obvious.

Many examples can be given. Every sin is a sin against the whole law and against all the commandments, although one is more explicit than the other.

All the commandments are given for all situations in life. That is true. But at the same time we have to keep in mind that the LORD gave us *ten* commandments and not just one. We have to make a distinction. When children disobey their parents, they transgress not only the fifth but also, for example, the eighth or the ninth commandment. But we consider it a transgression of the fifth commandment in the first place.

When an employee agrees with his employer to do a job and to follow his instructions, and when the employer agrees to pay him and to ensure that there are proper working conditions, both have to honour the contract. Any violation of the agreement is a sin against the ninth commandment. At the same time we realize that an employer who is negligent with respect to safety precautions sins against the sixth commandment (he willfully exposes his neighbour to a danger). On the other hand, an employee who idles away his time sins against the eighth commandment (he steals the time of his boss) and when he is unwilling to follow the instructions within the limits of the contract, he sins against the fifth commandment in being disobedient. The most obvious, however, is the ninth commandment.

15. Limited Reliability Company

In the past people considered ownership of a company to be equivalent to authority. However, that is not always and not necessarily the case.

In the production process three factors are important: capital, labour and resources. A company is often an agreement between the provider of the capital, the workers in the factory, and the supplier of the rough material (and, of course, the customers who are supposed to buy the product).

That ownership doesn't necessarily mean authority becomes clear in the case of a "silent partner" in a Limited Reliability Company. That is a company in which one partner has the money and the other the skills, the knowledge, the know-how or the salesmanship to run a business. By the very nature of the contract the owner shares in the profits, but he has little to say about the way the business is run. He puts his money in it and he trusts his companion. He is often not even able to run the business or to be involved in major decisions of management.

Another situation exists in a Limited Reliability Company with many shareholders. The Board of Management is in charge of the company, but basically the members of the Board are employees who are on the payroll. The real owners, the shareholders, do not have much "authority" in the daily decision making of the company.

With the modern trend of specialization, to run a business as a manager has become a profession in its own right. The manager depends for his management decisions on a staff of specialists. Sometimes the top advisors in technological development are payed more than the manager of the plant. Also here the law of supply and demand works. Modern business is a matter of teamwork and cooperation. Instead of one big boss, the owner, who makes all decisions, a staff of specialists works together. Then we cannot really speak about a situation of authority, in which the one is "higher" than the other, but we certainly can say that they all have to stick to their obligations, according to their mutual agreement. They have to fulfil their individual tasks according to the responsibilities given to them.

16. Conclusions

For us as Christians it is not of primary importance what rights we have and who is to be regarded as the greatest. That was the kind of questions the disciples were disputing among each other during the first celebration of the Lord's Supper (cf. Luke 22:24). We should follow the instruction of our Lord Jesus Christ and realize that we have to serve one another.

The Lord has given us a mandate in this world, to work to His glory, to use our gifts to the honour of His Name. We still have the opportunity to work and to take part in the labour process. There might come a time, and there willl come a time (according to Revelation 13), when Christians will be excluded from society. All over the world we can see the activities of "labour movements." Members of Labour unions call each other brothers and sisters. Let us be aware of our task and responsibility as Christians in this world. We should not take part in any revolutionary development, but work as citizens of the Kingdom of Heaven.

We have to be aware of the fact that, in all kinds of labour relations, there are old traditional patterns and opinions which are not based on the Word of God, but only on customs. We also have to realize that we are living in a time when the spirit of revolution and lawlessness is manifest everywhere.

Study of the Word of God is necessary to determine what our attitude should be. In this chapter I have tried to make a contribution to such a study. I hope that it will give some food for thought and discussion.

[1] Prof. B. Holwerda, *De crisis van het gezag* (Groningen, 1947), p.10.

————————— CHAPTER EIGHT —————————

Organized labour

1. A burning issue

On almost every newscast and in every newspaper we can hear and read about labour unrest. Strikes and lockouts are the order of the day. Picketlines can be seen everywhere. People who are on strike do not only picket their "own" company. There are also "secondary" picketings. Workers in other factories are also forced to stay away from their work site. Tensions sometimes run high, and violence often results. Workers who are glad that they can go back to work after months of unemployment are sometimes forced to go home again. Many families suffer financially and cannot make ends meet. Some have lost thousands of dollars of family income in a couple of months, not to mention the damage done to the national economy. Millions of dollars are lost, and sometimes lasting damage is caused by losing a market or missing some badly needed orders.

What must our attitude be to all this? How do we as Christians approach these problems? Even people who work in a non-union shop, because they have principle objections to union membership, are confronted with these problems. Recently, we saw that picket lines were set up also at non-union job sites. The attack will be intensified in the future. Non-union contractors have to be excluded from bidding in government orders and mega-projects. The troubles surrounding the construction of the "Expo 1986" world fair facilities, a multi-million project, are a clear example of it.

In this way also non-union workers can easily get involved in the struggle and must take a stand in these matters. A picket line is considered "sacred": crossing a picket line seems to be the most serious offence a worker can commit.

We have to consider our attitude and our response to these problems. The question of unionism is becoming a burning issue. To be "opposed to" unions is just not enough. We have to give a clear testimony *why* we are against it. An increasing number of people are beginning to question what is actually wrong with union membership. Some even say: it is required by law in some sectors of business life and therefore we have no choice. As law-abiding citizens we have to submit to the laws of the country.

Another point of discussion, and sometimes disagreement, is the question what the difference is between labour unions, trade associations, and products or marketing boards. Do we condemn membership of the one and condone membership of the other? Are "blue-collar" workers not allowed to have their unions while "white-collar" workers have their organizations, associations and boards to protect their rights, benefits and profits?

In this respect it is relevant to ask the question: what is the relationship between the employer and the employee? Is that a relationship of authority given by the Lord? Is what we read in Romans 13 and in Lord's Day 39 about authority and obedience applicable to the relationship between the employer and the employee? Do the workers have the right to organize themselves to take a stronger position in collective bargaining and to reach a more favourable contract, or is that a lack of respect for the "authorities" which are set over them? Do workers, "without gainsaying," have to obey the rules set by the "boss," with no other choice than to accept the wages and benefits offered by the employer or to leave and try to find another job? In the previous chapter we have already discussed some aspects of this issue.

These questions are very fundamental and we would do well to find an appropriate answer and take a clear stand in these matters. We should not just say "no" to a certain development or silently "accept" a certain obviously unavoidable course of actions. We have to examine the present situation by the light of the Word of God, and we have to prepare ourselves to explain and defend our position. Especially the younger generation is not served by telling them only that something is wrong, that we always have been opposed to it, and that it should stay that way. We have to convince our youth and sharpen our own mind, to be able to speak with the enemy in the gate. We have to give a clear testimony, also to those who are of a different opinion. We are supposed to be witnesses in this world. We are different from the people of the world in many aspects, we should be able to explain *why* we are different.

2. The purpose of our labour

In determining our attitude and formulating our point of view regarding the actual social issues, we first have to consider the meaning and purpose of all our labour. Why do we work? Why do we exert ourselves in our daily jobs as well as in all other activities? Is it just to make money, as much money as possible? Is it to get a promotion or to reach the highest rank on the social ladder?

A Christian should see his work and his daily task in a different way. It has to be the fulfilment of a divine mandate, in the first place. The Lord has created us and has given us a place on this earth to serve Him, to glorify His Name and to promote His Kingdom which is to come. Our labour has to bear fruits and has to be of value, not only in this life, but it has to be part of the service of the Lord that we take along into the New World. In Revelation 14:13 we read: "Blessed are the dead who die in the Lord from now on. 'Yes,' says the Spirit, 'they will rest from their labour, for their deeds will follow them.' " In the fifth petition we pray: "Give us this day our daily bread." According to Lord's Day 50 that means: "Provide us with all our bodily needs so that we may acknowledge that Thou art the only fountain of all good, and that our care and labour, and also Thy gifts, cannot do us any good without Thy blessing. Grant, therefore, that we may withdraw our trust from all creatures and place it alone in Thee."

Without the Lord's blessing neither our care and labour nor His gifts can profit us. All our labour is in vain if it is not done in obedience to the Lord and to His honour. The Lord provides for all our bodily needs. We have to acknowledge Him as the fountain of all good.

That puts our daily work in the right perspective. If we exert ourselves, spending all our time and energy in our work to reach our own goal, without asking what the Lord wants us to do, we cannot and should not expect His blessing on it. It is in vain. Although it might have great results and seem to yield great dividends, it does not really make sense or serve any real purpose.

We have to keep in mind this most important purpose and goal of life when we discuss our attitude with respect to our daily task and responsibility in this world.

3. Authority and obedience

Another aspect we have to consider is the relationship between employer and employee. In chapter VII we already noted that the relationship between employer and employee in our modern society is completely different from that of slaves and their masters in the time of the Old Testament; it is also different from the position of slaves in the time of the apostle Paul. Slaves were members of the household of the master. They were subject to the authority of their masters, the head of the family, and often the head of the community in legal and judicial matters. The master's authority was a combination of what we nowadays see as the governing authorities, according to Romans 13, and the authority given to parents, referred to in the fifth commandment.

In our modern society we have an agreement between employer and employee which is the result of free negotiations. Such a contract can be continued or terminated by both parties, according to the terms set out in the contract.

Any unfaithfulness, disobedience or other breach of contract is a sin against the *ninth* commandment: we should keep our promises and stick to our commitments. It is also a sin against the *eighth* commandment: we must promote our neighbour's good wherever we can and may, and deal with him as we would like others to deal with us. That applies both ways. The employee has made a commitment to do his work according to the instructions given by his supervisor. Any disobedience or unfaithfulness on his part is a breach of contract. The employer has the duty to provide proper working conditions, to protect his workers against any danger on the worksite, and to pay fair wages. When an employer fails to do these things, or is unfaithful in another way, he is also guilty of breaking the contract.

Unfortunately, both parties are not always willing to do their share. Sometimes one of the parties involved abuses his position to force the other to do something which is not according to the contract. This leads to conflict situations, resulting in fights between employers and employees. Both seek their strength with their colleagues, joining the battle either in an organization of employers or an organization of employees.

4. Abuse of power

Many examples can be mentioned of abuse of power. In the nineteenth century labour was very "cheap," and readily available, and the workers had little choice but to accept the terrible working conditions and extremely low wages. The employers had all the power in the world, and they often abused their position to make large profits at the cost of their employees. In some industries people had to work sixteen or eighteen hours a day; even children had to work fourteen hours a day. The working conditions were sometimes very bad and unhealthy, and the wages were so low that parents could hardly keep their children alive and provide food for them, let alone pay for proper housing and clothing. However, they had no choice but to accept the situation. Some employers and company owners abused their powerful position.

Fortunately, there were also employers who really cared for their people and provided them with proper wages and benefits. However, in general, it was a very difficult time for many workers. We should not ignore these past developments. They were a stimulus to the organized labour movement.

5. Labour organizations

What is our attitude regarding labour organizations? Do we condemn all organizations set up by workers to defend their rights over against the position of their employers? Certainly not!

The labour movement in this part of the world has followed a different route than in Europe. At the beginning of this century — in 1905, to be more precise, — a Christian Social Congress was organized in the Netherlands. At this congress the following statement was made: "The purpose of a labour organization is to help the workers in their aim for a better legal position in their branch of industry and to provide such labour regulations that will enable them to fulfil their God-given calling, for the development of their own strength and gifts as well as for their families, their branch of industry, the country and the church." This is a rather lengthy sentence, but the meaning is clear. A Christian labour organization had to be established whose aim it was to secure a better legal position and to provide fair labour regulations. Its ultimate purpose was that the workers be better equipped to fulfil their God-given calling, for the benefit of their families, the country and the church.

Over against the socialistic labour movement, based upon the principle of revolution and "class war," a Christian organization structure was established. The socialists had taken over the "class war" idea from Karl Marx. He propagated the ongoing struggle between capital and labour, between capitalists and labourers, between the rich and the poor, between oppressors and the oppressed. The Christian labour movement, however, sought to reach its goal through reasonable and peaceful negotiations. It was the "harmony model" as opposed to the "conflict model."

This development shows us that there is basically nothing wrong with having a labour organization, or against working together as labourers in a certain trade to get better legal protection or to reach a better contract in collective negotiations. The question is how this aim is reached and what means are used.

6. Different types of organizations

A labour movement can be organized in different ways. In the past, already as early as the Middle Ages, there were "guilds." A guild was an association of businessmen and skilled workers who joined together to help one another and to make rules for training new members. The main purpose of a guild was to maintain a high level of skill and workmanship, not to negotiate contracts between employers and employees. In such guilds both employers and employees were represented.

In some countries the labour movement is organized along political or religious lines. In the Netherlands, for instance, there is a socialistic labour union, a Roman Catholic union and a Christian labour union. The socialistic and Roman Catholic unions are joined together in one organization. Each union is divided into sections for the different branches of industry. There are not only organizations of employees but also organization of employers. Both have their own "union"; the labour contracts that are drawn up are collective settlements between the organization of employers and the organization of employees. Union membership is not mandatory. There are no closed shops. Everyone is free to join or not to join a union, and everyone is free to join the union of his choice. In almost every large company the three big unions are represented.

There is even a Reformed organization, called GMV which stands for Gereformeerd Maatschappelijk Verbond (= Reformed Social Alliance). In this organization employers and employees work together. Many members of the Reformed Churches in the Netherlands are organized in this union, and in a number of companies it is officially recognized as a trade union.

In Canada, however, the unions are organized per branch of industry, and in one particular company there is only one union. Besides, union membership is mandatory. If a company is "unionized," all employees *have* to join the union. The company is not allowed to hire people who are not willing to join the union, and sometimes people who have been employed for a long time already, have to be laid off. Later we will go into more detail on the structure of labour unions. Now we will first take a look at the different types of organizations which are required by law.

7. Legislative regulations

A really confusing and sometimes controversial issue is the difference between a labour union, a trade association, a products board, a marketing board, and the like. Since some are established by law, some people say: "We, as law-abiding citizens, have to comply with the law. We have to participate in such organizations, whether we like it or not. It is just like paying taxes: although you might not like it and consider it to be unfair, you have to pay."

Others say: "if you are allowed to participate in a product or a marketing board and pay your share, because it is law, why may we not pay our union fee, if that is mandatory?"

Another group reasons just the other way around and says: "If you disapprove of membership in a trade union and ask people to look for a non-union job, then you should also disapprove of participation in marketing boards, products boards and trade associations. We should not make a difference between 'blue-collar' and 'white-collar' workers in this respect. We have to obey the law, but we can also avoid a confrontation with the law by looking for another job. If, for instance, it would become law that every nurse has to assist in performing abortions, it would become necessary for nurses to seek another job."

This reasoning sounds appealing and it has a certain merit. From the Book of Revelation (chapter 13) we learn that there will come a time of persecution and boycott for those who believe in Jesus Christ and obey the Word of God. There will come a separation between those who bear the sign of Jesus Christ, the Lamb of God, and those who have the mark of the beast upon their forehead and upon their right hand. In some, and probably in an increasing number of professions, there will be no place for Christians. That is what the Bible teaches us and we had better be prepared for that.

However, more has to be said. Not all organizations are alike. We have seen already that a labour movement as such is not necessarily wrong. That employees work together to protect their own position and to get a better contract is a legitimate cause. The question is: How do they achieve their aim? What kind of means do they use?

Before we answer these questions, we must take a closer look at the structure of labour unions.

8. The nature of the commitment

Before we reject a certain organization and condemn those who join it, we should first study its constitution to see how they reach their goal.

Products boards and marketing boards are established by law. Sometimes the members are appointed by the Governor-in-Council or by the Minister of Agriculture, as is the case, for instance, with the Canadian Dairy Commission (Act R.S.C. 1970, c. C-7). Sometimes an existing committee is authorized and empowered by the Governor-in-Council, as, for instance, with the Agricultural Products Marketing Boards and Agencies (Act R.S.C 1970, c. A-7) or by another cabinet minister, as with the Canadian Wheat Board (Act R.S.C. 1970, c. C-12). Such boards can have power and authority "to fix, impose and collect levies or charges from persons engaged in production or marketing of the whole or part of any agricultural product." That means that the producers and sellers of certain products have to pay a levy. They are obliged by law to do so. However, that is nothing more than paying a "tax."

It is a different story with trade associations. Sometimes voluntary or mandatory membership is involved to be allowed to work in a certain profession. Then the question has to be asked what form of commitment is required in order to join the association. What does the constitution say and how is it practiced? There may be no unacceptable obligation or commitment. It is also possible, however, that membership causes a conflict situation and that commitments are required which cannot be made by a Christian. Careful consideration is necessary and every case has to be taken on its own merits. It is impossible within the framework of this chapter to go into detail about all the possibilities.

9. Total commitment

I will mention one example to show what the nature of a labour unions is. It is not just another association of workers in a certain profession; it is an organization which requires complete allegiance and total commitment. It is almost a religion. For many it is even more than a religion. People trust in their union.

We confess in Lord's Day 50 that the Lord is the only fountain of all good, and that our care and labour, and also His gifts, cannot do us any good without His blessing. We therefore withdraw our trust from all creatures and place it only in the Lord.

Union members, however, put their trust in their union. "Solidarity for ever and the Union makes us strong," they sing. Union members call each other "brothers and sisters." They have a form for the installation of officers, which is very similar to the form for the installation of office-bearers in the church. In an appendix to the constitution of one of the unions I found the recommended text for the ritual of installation of officers. It begins as follows: "You have been selected by your brothers and sisters to fill the different offices of this local union. We shall now proceed to the installation of the officers." Then the question is asked: "Do you solemnly pledge your word of honour in the presence of this meeting, that you will, to the best of your ability, discharge all the duties incumbent upon you as an officer of a local union . . . ." In the recommended text we further read phrases like: "Fill your office well and leave it with honour. He or she who has risen to office has done well; he or she who has risen in office has done better. May the better part be yours . . . . Therefore, be faithful to the office you have been elected to fill . . . be zealous in your office . . . . One who is faithful in that which is least is also faithful in what is much. Be faithful." This shows clearly how close it is to a religion. Almost the same words and phrases are used and the same commitments have to be made.

Eligible members, before being admitted to full membership, shall subscribe to the following obligation: "I_____(name) pledge my honour to faithfully observe the Constitution and the laws of this Union;

to comply with all the rules and regulations for the government thereof; not to divulge or make known any private proceedings of this Union; to faithfully perform all the duties assigned to me; that I will not wrong a member, or see him or her wronged, if in my power to prevent; to so conduct myself at all times as not to bring reproach upon my Union, and at all times to bear true and faithful allegiance to the . . . Union."

The whole formulation and setup of the procedure shows that the union requires the complete and full allegiance of its members.

In Lord's Day 42, Answer 111, of the Heidelberg Catechism, we confess that the eighth commandment requires: "I must promote my neighbour's good wherever I can and may, deal with him as I would like others to deal with me." Unions require the same from their members — not with respect to their "neighbours," but only with respect to their brothers and sisters in the union.

In Lord's Day 47, Answer 122, we pray the Lord to grant "that we may so direct our whole life — our thoughts, words, and actions — that Thy Name is not blasphemed because of us but always honoured and praised." Unions require that their members conduct themselves at all times as not to bring reproach upon their union, and that at all times they bear true and faithful allegiance to their union.

Before a Christian can make such a commitment, the consequences have to be considered. When someone has to "pledge his honour to faithfully observe the Constitution and laws of a union" and "to comply with all the rules and regulations for the government thereof," the question has to be asked what this commitment means. What are these "rules and regulations?"

The most important and far-reaching rule is that every member of the union is obligated to participate in a strike, as soon as such a strike is approved by the national president or by the national executive board. About those who refuse to participate the constitution says: "Any member having accepted employment in any place in which a strike has been approved by the National President shall, by this act, expel himself from membership in the National Union."

Union members also have the obligation to walk the picket line, if requested to do so, and failure to perform picket duty is considered to be contrary to the Constitution and therefore a serious offence. Disciplinary actions can be taken against such a member, "which may include fine, suspension, removal from office or expulsion from membership."

Before we deal with the question whether a Christian can make such a commitment, we first will have a closer look at what a strike is.

10. On strike

When we consider the question whether we can participate in a strike, we have to make a distinction between the legal and the moral aspects.

A strike is a phenomenon that existed already as early as the Middle Ages. The oldest strike I have heard about was in 1372. Textile workers went on strike in the city of Leiden in the Netherlands. However, the strike was illegal. Strong sentences were meted out to those who participated in, or who incited others to participate in, the strike. Even the death penalty was used. During, and especially at the end of, the nineteenth century there was a different approach. The labour movement became active and the regulations about strikes were mitigated. Slowly a strike became a legally accepted phenomenon.

In Canada strikes are legal, at least if certain conditions are met. We often hear that a union or the workers in a certain branch of industry are "in a legal position to strike." The same can be said about the employers. In some instances they have the right to "lock out" the workers in a certain workplace. In both cases the workers leave the worksite and do not receive their pay-cheque. Although this might be legally permissible, that does not mean that it is also morally right. A number of pages back we saw that the purpose of our daily work is not in the first place to make money. It is the fulfilment of our God-given mandate.

Earlier I have referred to the abuse of power. In the past it happened that employers abused their powerful position to make lots of money at the cost of the workers who lived in very poor conditions, on the point of starvation, and who had to work hard in very bad and unhealthy conditions. We should not ignore or deny these facts, or try to condone them. It has been one of the reasons for the establishment of labour organizations.

However, what we see happening today is also the abuse of powerful position. There is an old saying which goes: "someone else's dirt is not our soap." It means that we should not use the mistakes and wrongdoings of others to excuse our own actions or to whitewash and defend our own mistakes. I do not see anything wrong with labourers' joining and working together to get a better deal and a more favourable contract. However, the question is what means they use to reach their goal.

There are different aspects about a strike which make it an unacceptable tool for us to reach the goal. In the first place it is a denial of our God-given mandate to labour faithfully. The daily process of labour is interrupted to force others to give in to demands which otherwise cannot be reached. That is an abuse of a powerful position. People talk about "solidarity," but this solidarity is often only a matter of putting pressure on other workers to support a certain case, whether they like it or not. Workers are threatened, and even violence is used for those who are not willing to participate in the revolutionary actions. Recently, I saw that the worksite of a non-union company was closed by picket lines. Workers who want nothing to do with unions are prevented from doing their work. Equipment is damaged and personal injury is caused.

We have to reject such revolutionary actions. They have nothing to do with democracy but are a step on the way to anarchy. Even the laws of the country are violated. A small group of people tries to impose its will on the rest of society.

It is clear that such actions are illegal, but also many "legal" strikes are morally unacceptable. It is not just a matter of the abuse of a powerful position. It can put a great burden on innocent people. A strike sometimes costs millions of dollars. This burden has to be carried not only by the workers and their employers. Lots of other people suffer as well. When there is a transit strike, the general public suffers in the first place. A strike of public workers causes a lot of problems for the public. A strike of hospital workers can even endanger human life and health. And the irony of the case is that the workers often lose more money while on strike than they stand to gain during the whole term of their new contract.

We face a revolutionary development which defeats its purpose. No wonder that there is an increasing unhappiness and dissatisfaction with the work of the unions. The aversion to this development can be seen in many sectors of industry.

We, as Christians, must take a strong stand against these actions. We do not defend or condone the abuse of power on the part of the employers, as it has happened in the past. There was a good reason for workers to defend their rights and to work together for the improvement of their working conditions. But the way the labour unions are working now is certainly no good alternative. It is simply the other extreme.

11. Serving two masters

In section 9 of this chapter I explained the character of the personal commitment of the members to their union. It is a full allegiance. I quoted, as an example, the "subscription form" of a certain union. Every member has to "pledge his honour to faithfully observe the Constitution and laws of the Union; to comply with all the rules and regulations for the government thereof." To comply with these rules and regulations includes to go on strike if the national executive board decides to do so. It also includes the duty to "honour" the picket lines of all other unions and to perform picket duty if requested to do so.

Some people might say: "I *have* to join a union to get a certain job. I have no choice. But I am not going to participate in a strike or to walk the picket line. If they ever ask me to do so I will quit my job. But for the time being I am just paying my fee and I do not want any trouble. If the time comes, I will see."

However, that does not solve the problem. If someone "pledges his honour to faithfully observe the Constitution and the laws of the Union and to comply with all the rules and regulations for the government thereof," he has to keep his promise and to be faithful to his "word of honour." It is simply not fair to the Union, and it is even in conflict with the ninth commandment of the Law of the Lord, to make such a pledge with the clear intention of not sticking to it.

In Matthew 6:24 Jesus warned us, saying: "No one can serve two masters; for either he will hate the one and love the other, or he will be devoted to the one and despise the other. You cannot serve God and mammon." A Christian cannot make the full commitment which the unions ask of their members, and *at the same time* commit his whole life in true obedience to the Lord. We cannot serve two masters. Either someone is faithful in his commitment to the union and his "brothers and sisters" in the labour movement (but then he has to put the word of men above the Word of

God), or he is faithful in his commitment to the Lord and His service (but then he can not "comply with all the rules and regulations" of the union). We cannot serve two masters! Either we will "hate the one and love the other" or we will "be devoted to the one and despise the other" (cf. Matthew 6:24).

Our conclusion must be that union membership, as mentioned above, is incompatible with membership of the Church of Jesus Christ.

12. Other organizations

There is still one point that needs our attention, and that is our attitude toward all kinds of trade associations, products and marketing boards, and the like.

There is a wide spectrum of organizations. It is impossible to go into detail on all of them. In dealing with the matter of labour unions, I took one particular labour union as an example and quoted from its official constitution. There might be some differences in the constitutions of the various unions. Some are more, others less, demanding. Some require their members to take an oath; others only require a written application for membership and there is no mention of an "oath" on the application form. Others might even consider a verbal agreement and payment of the fees sufficient for becoming a member. The all-important consideration, however, is what the official constitution says about the obligations of the members of an organization.

Most products and marketing boards are appointed by a cabinet minister or by the Governor-in-Council. They receive their power and authority by law from the civil government. The producers and sellers (or marketeers) of certain products have to pay a levy set by the government. As long as no other obligations are involved or are incumbent upon the "members," I can see nothing unacceptable about these rules. I even wonder whether the term "members" can be used in this case. At least in some instances nothing more than the payment of something like a sales tax is involved. However, if other obligations are attached, they have to be considered on their own merits.

The same counts for some trade associations and other organizations of workers in a certain area of science or technology. If it is just an organization to exchange know-how and experience and to administer matters of common interest, it is not necessarily wrong to participate in such an association. The main point remains: What does the constitution say and what are the obligations of the members? Careful scrutiny is always necessary. Experience has taught that cooperation in many such organisations, which from the outset seemed to be very innocent, became difficult because of the spirit of revolution and lawlessness which crept in.

Let us be on the alert and let us help each other in these difficult times. The spirit of revolution is active. We have to fight, not in the first place against flesh and blood, but against "the wiles of the devil" (cf. Ephesians 6:10-20). It might be a difficult task, but we have sure protection: the whole armour of God. The sword of the Spirit and the Word of God are our weapons. Counting on the promises given to us in Ephesians 6, we can overcome. May this chapter be of some help in studying these matters as a training for the battle.

CHAPTER NINE

Our position on lotteries

1. They are everywhere

Today we are confronted with lotteries everywhere in one way or another. Grocery stores as well as gas stations offer you tickets which can make you an instant cash winner. In almost every store or shopping mall you can either buy draw tickets or get them free. When you subscribe to a magazine or order a book, you receive a ticket which can make you an instant winner. Lotteries and sweepstakes are used for sales promotion as well as to encourage people to make a donation to a charitable organization. The government uses lotteries to collect funds to subsidise sport events and other activities. "Chance" games are used to attract people to and amuse them at fairs. Lottery tickets are also sold simply to satisfy people who love gambling. Lots of money which should have been used in the household for the most basic necessities, is spent buying lottery tickets, because people are captivated by the idea that they could win the big "jackpot." Many people have become addicted to lotteries.

I have been asked to write about this matter, because there are differences of opinion among us on it. We are so bombarded by lotteries that it has become very difficult to steer clear of it. Most of us agree that gambling is wrong. The old version of the Form for the Lord's Supper says that gamblers should stay away from the table of the Lord. However, what is gambling? Some reason that taking part in a lottery or draw is not wrong, as long as the tickets are free. Others see nothing wrong with having a "draw" at a fund-raising bazaar for a Christian school. And when do we call it a real lottery? Only when you buy a ticket with a number on it, or also when you "guess" the number of peas in a pot or the weight of a cake at a bazaar? Usually you do not get a free ticket for these events, but you have to pay for it!

In this chapter I will try to deal with this matter in an orderly and principled way. I will investigate what the Bible says about it, what the attitude has been among Reformed people in the past, and what our approach should be in the present situation.

I will not restrict myself to the most common form of sweepstakes, lotteries and gambling. I will also pay attention to other forms of "gambling" such as excessive participation in the stock market and dealing with "futures" and other "high-risk" investments. Isn't speculation via the stock market simply a more sophisticated way of gambling?

2. What is "the lot"?

In the Bible we often read that the lot was cast. The key text in this respect is Proverbs 16:33, where it says: "The lot is cast into the lap, but the decision is wholly from the Lord." In the New Testament we read in Luke 1:9 that, according to the custom, it fell to Zechariah by lot to enter the temple of the LORD and burn incense. In Acts 1:26 we read about the election of an apostle. They cast lots, and the lot fell on Matthias. We do not know exactly what procedure they followed, but it is clear that the lot was used to decide in certain matters and that the decision came from the Lord. That is what Proverbs 16:33 says.

A well-known Reformed professor in ethics, Dr. W. Geesink, in his book *Gereformeerde Ethiek* (Reformed Ethics), distinguishes three different types of situations in which the lot was used. The first is *revelation*. The LORD made special revelations to His people via the Urim and the Thummim (e.g. Exodus 28:30). Another use of the lot was *consultation*. In difficult matters the LORD was asked to decide. When the people of Israel were defeated in the battle against the people of Ai, Joshua had to bring the whole congregation before the LORD and the LORD Himself pointed out who the transgressor was that had brought down the wrath of the Lord on the whole congregation. A third type of situation in which the lot was used according to Prof. Geesink, is a case of *division*. Here he refers to situations in which something had to be divided among persons; situations in which something had to be allotted, allocated or apportioned. That was the case when the people had to divide the promised land or when the services of the priests in the temple had to be allotted, as we can learn from Luke 1:9 concerning Zechariah.

In the Bible we also read about unbelievers who used the lot to come to a decision. A well-known example is that of Haman who cast the lot to find out what would be the best time to destroy the Jewish people (Esther 3:7). In Jonah 1:7 we read that the people who were with Jonah cast the lot to find out on whose account the storm had arisen. And, to mention just one more, in John 19:24 we read about the soldiers, who cast the lot over Jesus' tunic, to see whose it would be. With their evil deeds they fulfilled the prophecy of Psalm 22:18: "They divide my garments among them, and for my raiment they cast lots."

From all these examples it is clear that the lot has been used throughout the ages, by believers as well as unbelievers. However, the question has to be answered whether we, as Christians, are allowed to use the lot and in what circumstances it is proper to do so.

3. A classic opinion

In the previous section I made a reference to what Prof. Geesink wrote about the lot. He distinguishes three different categories, which he calls *revelation, consultation,* and *division.* He considers the first and the second to belong to the Old Dispensation, and therefore not to be used by Christians. The only way we are allowed to use the lot is in making a choice in cases of "division," for instance with an inheritance, or when a choice has to be made between persons, as in an election. Another case of making a choice is mentioned in Proverbs 18:18. When there is a dispute, in which it is very difficult to decide, the lot can be used. "The lot puts an end to disputes and decides between powerful contenders." In some churches the lot is used for the election of office-bearers. In some congregations there is the rule that when there is a tie vote the oldest is considered chosen; in other places they use the lot to break a tie.

Prof. Geesink is of the opinion that the lot can rightly be used in such situations. However, the use of the lot should always be a serious, well-considered request to the Lord to decide in a matter which seems too difficult for us to decide on. That is why he considers it disrespectful to use the lot during a game to decide whose turn it is to play, and even more so to ask the Lord to decide who will win the jackpot. Prof. Geesink is very consistent in applying this rule. He strongly opposes all forms of lotteries and card playing. He also condemns the use of dice, no matter what the game might be. His reasoning is that in such cases we are asking the Lord to decide on something we are doing just for fun. That, according to him, is showing a lack of respect for the decisions of the Lord and is a profaning of His Name. The use of the lot is permitted, but it should always be done in the awareness that we call upon the Name of the Lord. Preferably it should be done with prayer, as is the case when we use the lot during an election of office-bearers to break a tie.

Prof. Geesink even goes so far as to condemn all games in which an element of "luck" is involved or where things happen "by accident." He writes (vol. 1, page 342): "On the same grounds as card and dice games, also domino and lotto games have to be condemned." This means that almost all our board games are unacceptable - not only the games in which dice are used, but also games like Scrabble, because, just as with the old domino game, it is a matter of "luck" what letters you get with which to play the game. According to Prof. Geesink, it is disrespectful to have the Lord decide how "lucky" you will be in a game. He even says that during such a game the player "hopes" or "prays" that the Lord may cause him to win the game. He considers it ethically unacceptable that we ask the Lord to decide on so-called "contingent" matters in such a way that we gain something at the cost of a friend with whom we are playing a game.

So far the opinion of a very prominent professor in ethics at the beginning of this century. His opinion was certainly no exception. It represented the classic approach to this problem among Reformed people. Before we come to an evaluation of this point of view and a formulation of our own opinion, we will first have a closer look at some other aspects of this matter.

4. Different types of lotteries

All kinds of names are used, like sweepstakes, lotto, etc., and these terms are often used interchangeable, in a confusing way, as if they were synonymous. What is the difference? I will list the most common words and define them.

Sweepstakes is a gaming transaction in which a number of people contribute a certain amount of money, their "stake," with the understanding that the total amount becomes the property of one or some of them under certain, previously accepted conditions. It was originally used at horse races, where people could set an amount of money on a horse, hoping that this horse would win. In the event that their horse won, they would collect the total amount or "sweep the stakes." The most typical element is that the outcome is determined by an uncertain *event in the future*. It is a form of "betting." Nowadays the name *sweepstakes* is used for all kinds of lotteries, also when they are not determined by an event in the future and when no "stakes" are set.

A *lottery* is a game or method of fund raising in which tickets are sold and in which certain ticket holders are entitled to a prize. In a draw by chance, the winners are determined. Here the main point is that tickets are sold and that the outcome does not depend on a more or less predictable fact, but on a *draw by chance* or casting of the lot.

Lotto or *bingo* is a game in which certain numbers in a row or circle have to be covered or chosen. Here the outcome depends on the way the *player himself fills in* his card or ticket.

A *bet* is a pledge made on the result of some uncertain questions or events. The bettor receives a reward if his prediction comes true. Here the question who gets the money depends on the *correctness of the "prediction"* or expectation of the bettor.

Roulette is a game of chance in which the winner is determined by a moving ball, which drops into a numbered compartment of a *spinning disk*. Each player places his bet on one of the compartments.

Gambling, in general, is a venture in which a great risk is taken solely for the purpose of gaining money. The most characteristic element of gambling is not only that the risk of losing money is accepted, but that *taking the risk is an aim in itself.*

Speculation is a special type of gambling. It is a financial investment which is hazardous but offers the possibility of large profits. It can be done by buying and selling risky shares on the stock market. It can also be done by dealing in "futures." This is the technical term for buying or selling commodities or stocks on the basis of delivery in the future. A businessman, for instance, can sell a product on the basis of delivery after half a year. If he is convinced that the price of this product will decrease dramatically, he can sell the product for a fixed price, even if he does not have it available as yet, because he hopes to be able to buy or grow it for a reasonable price before the delivery date is due. However, if the price goes up in the meantime, he can lose a lot of money because, in order to stick to his contract, he has to buy for a higher price than he has already sold. This is a very common form of "gambling," and some people who know the market can make a lot of money in this way, while many have lost everything by this form of speculation. In our evaluation we will also consider this form of gambling.

5. Taking risks

To take risks is part of business life. A farmer has to decide on the best time for sowing or planting. If he starts early, he takes the risk that frost will destroy his crop. If he is late, he takes the risk that his product will reach the market at a time when prices are very low. The greater the risk he takes, the more he stands to gain or lose. However, if he does not take any risks, he will never make it in business life. In Ecclesiastes 11:4 we read: "He who observes the wind will never sow; and he who regards the clouds will never reap." A sales manager has to decide when and how much he has to order. Buying too little can cause him to run out of stock and lose the opportunity to sell. Ordering too much leaves him with unsold stock.

As I said, taking risks is part of business life. It can be attractive for a farmer to sell his whole crop under contract at the beginning of the season. It gives him a certain guarantee that he will sell his products for a reasonable price. If he waits, the prices may go up, and he can make more money, but if the prices go down, he has gained by selling in advance.

These kinds of risks have to be considered by every businessman. This has led to the "futures market." Some producers like to sell their products in advance, in order to help them plan and to be sure that they can sell for a reasonable price. Others are willing to buy in advance, accepting the risk that the price may go up or down in the meantime. Such a business deal is not necessarily wrong.

The same counts for investments. A person who has to invest a large amount of money, either for himself or for a company or an organization, has to consider the profits or the returns of his investment. The safest way to invest is not always the most profitable. Shares in companies which make large profits one year are more likely to devaluate in another year than more conservative investments. The greater the profit or return of an investment, the greater often the risk that money will be lost. Professional investors, such as trust companies, have a certain formula to spread the risk over different types of investment. That is what business life is all about. And again I have to say that there is nothing wrong with taking a certain, well-considered risk, in order to get a reasonable return.

Speculation, however, we must reject, since it is a form of gambling. What is the difference? Let me put it this way: the risk to be taken should be in reasonable proportion to the type of business one is in and should be part of it. That a farmer sells his crop in advance or a factory buys the products they need on the "futures market" is not gambling. Nor is it gambling when a trust company or a pension fund invests a certain portion of its money in medium or high-risk shares on the stock market. That is part of proper financial management. However, if someone who is not involved in a certain line of trade or business buys or sells "futures" for the simple reason that he hopes to gain a lot of money if the prices go up, he is gambling. Too many have lost a fortune with this type of gambling.

It is the same with buying and selling at the stock market. When someone puts all his money in a certain very risky fund, hoping that he will get a large profit, he is gambling. There is a general rule among investors which states that one should never be involved in a high-risk enterprise with money that one cannot afford to lose. It means that the savings of an average family should not be used to invest in high-risk stocks or bonds. That would be gambling. However, a large company can invest a certain amount of money in an undertaking which is not guaranteed to be successful. That is what we mean by saying that the risk must be in proportion to the type of business and should be part of the business.

Speculation is taking risks which are out of proportion or which have nothing to do with one's trade or line of business. It is taking risks for the sole purpose of taking risks.

6. Games

Having mentioned the different types of gambling and lottery and having seen that even taking risks in business can become a matter of "gambling," we will have a closer look at different types of games.

In section 3 I already mentioned that in the past there were people who were of the opinion that any form of "chance" in a game was wrong. Not only a game in which dice are used, but even a game like Scrabble was not allowed. The reason was that the outcome depends on how "lucky" you are with the cards, dominoes or letters you get.

I think this goes too far. It is certainly true that in a game like Scrabble the outcome to a certain extent depends on what letters you get by "chance." And we know that the hand of the Lord is in everything in our life and that nothing happens without His will. However, I do not think that anyone "prays" that the Lord will grant him a favourable set of letters in the game. That would be an idle use of the Name of the Lord.

The criterion in this whole matter is the question what the motives are. As long as it is only a pastime, I do not see the element of "chance" in a Scrabble game as "gambling." The same applies to other board games. However, as soon as we use the lot or dice to decide in a matter which we consider to be important, it is not a simple "game" or pastime anymore. If the outcome is important and is more than just a matter of amusement, we pass the borderline between what is gambling and what is not. Some say that there is nothing wrong with using lots, as long as you do not have to pay for it. This, in my opinion, is not correct. The question is not whether you have to pay for your "ticket," your "chance" or your "card"; the criterion should be whether we are playing only for the joy of playing or for the prize. As soon as the "prize" becomes important, we are on the wrong track. Then we bring ourselves into the temptation of greed for gain.

This is basically the same as with taking risks in business and gambling on the stock market. As soon as gaining money or winning something by chance becomes the purpose, we are on a path which contradicts the tenth commandment.

Nowadays we can receive lottery (draw) tickets everywhere for free.

People are often very surprised when you say that you do not want a draw ticket. "Don't you want to win a prize?" they ask.

However, we must be consistent and be aware of the danger. If we participate in this modern rage of lotteries and draws, we do not only expose ourselves to the *temptation* of "coveting," against the tenth commandment, but we have already become involved in this activity. The apostle Paul says in I Timothy 6:9,10: "But those who desire to be rich fall into temptation, into a snare, into many senseless and hurtful desires that plunge men into ruin and destruction. For the love of money is the root of all evils; it is through this craving that some have wandered away from the faith and pierced their hearts with many pang⊆."

Let us as Christians show self-control also in this respect. We can easily be led astray by the fact that everyone does it. However, the Lord teaches us that the love of money is the *root* of all evils. And the apostle Paul adds to his warning (I Timothy 6:11): "But as for you, man of God, shun all this."

7. Conclusions

We have seen that in all kinds of games "chance" plays a role — not only in board games in which dice are used, but also in dominoes and Scrabble. In the past the Reformed point of view was, at least according to Prof. Geesink's *Reformed Ethics*, that any game in which "chance" is involved had to be condemned. I do not believe that in a game like Scrabble or dominoes we are profaning the Name of the Lord and are asking Him every time to decide how "lucky" we will be. We do see a great danger in the present rage of lotteries, sweepstakes, and lottos, which is coming over us. Too many are participating in such lotteries without realizing where the borderline lies between playing a game as pastime on the one hand and gambling on the other. The criterion should not be whether we have to pay for our ticket. Very often the price of the ticket is included in the price of the product you buy, and so you are paying for it anyway. Neither should the criterion be whether it is for a good purpose. Even the big provincial or national lotteries are often played to support a good purpose. The only correct criterion, as far as I can see, is the question whether winning a prize is the *purpose* of the game, or whether it is a matter of amusement, entertainment — a pastime. As soon as the result gives us "profit," it becomes a matter of "greed for goods." And then we should not use the lot to decide who will get the prize. I agree with Prof. Geesink that the lot can be used as a means to decide in matters of division, but only in the proper way; that is, with calling upon the Name of the Lord, as is sometimes the case with the elections of office-bearers.

Taking risks in business life, as is the case on the stock market with buying and selling shares and bonds or with the so-called "futures market," is not necessarily wrong, as long as it is part of someone's business and as long as the risks are in proportion with the line of trade or business. It becomes gambling as soon as the risk-taking becomes an aim in itself.

It is very important to think about these things and to set a clear criterion. Otherwise we will end up with a floating borderline which drifts away very easily and will be adjusted by everyone according to his or her individual circumstances. Let us not forget the warning in Jeremiah 17:9: "The heart is deceitful above all things, and desperately corrupt; who can understand it?" It may be worthwhile to discuss these matters in the Bible study societies, to help each other develop a Scriptural point of view. I hope that this chapter will contribute to a fruitful discussion.

CHAPTER TEN

The influence of the news media

1. Our daily dose

Every day we are confronted with world news in one way or another. We hear it on the radio, watch it on T.V. or read it in our daily newspaper. We all know that there are bad T.V. programs, and therefore we must be careful about what we watch, if we watch at all. Most people feel, however, that the daily newscast is the only program, or almost the only program, you can watch without being afraid of a bad influence. After all, the news gives only the facts, the reality. Although it is not always nice to see the news, it shows what life is all about. With other programs we have to be careful that we do not get indoctrinated, but with the news we only receive factual information. At least, that is what most people think.

I am not so sure about that. I agree that many, if not all, "entertainment" programs have a bad influence on the viewers. Too much time is spent watching this medium and little, if anything, is gained from it. Few people are aware of the danger of T.V. and the way it infiltrates our homes and dominates the lives of so many. The sad consequences are evident, but it seems almost impossible to stop this process. T.V. has received its place also in Christian homes.

In this chapter I will not deal, in the first place, with the bad influence of the modern entertainment programs in general. Others may be better qualified to do so. What I would like to achieve is to show that also the so-called "objective" newscasts are not as innocent as they may seem to be, but that they are giving us a daily dose of indoctrination.

It is very important how the news is presented. The public is manipulated, not only by the commentators who are supposed to give background information and who are asked for their opinions, but also by the reporters who seem to give plain "news." Did you ever notice that the very presence of the media has an impact on the course of events? Demonstrations and walkouts in public schools in the Vancouver area were a clear example. As soon as the students learned that the media were present, they really started their demonstration and became excited. The fact that there is news coverage makes the public more aggressive. I am not suggesting that media personnel purposely incite people to stage violent demonstrations. That might happen the odd time, but it would be wrong to blame all the news media in general for the wrongs of some. However, it is an undeniable fact that the presence of a T.V. camera works as a catalyst for many people.

And there is more we have to consider. The presentation by the news media is not always as objective as it is presumed to be. The newscast is catered to the wishes of the viewers. The length of time allocated to the coverage of a particular event is in accordance with the importance of the event in the eyes of the media, or rather, in accordance with what they think the public likes to hear.

What determines how important an event is? Not the number of people involved. The importance of a demonstration is not measured by the number of participants. Sometimes extensive coverage is given to a very small demonstration. Some newsmen (purposely) manipulate their audience. But even when they do not intend to manipulate public opinion, they *are* catering to what they see as the average consumer. The time-slot allocated to a certain issue in the news is often measured in seconds, but when a hockey game is covered, all other regularly scheduled programs are preempted and hours are spent on coverage of the game. Apparently, the program directors are of the opinion that the majority of people want to see this rather than the regular programs. Even the regularly scheduled newscasts are cancelled for a game.

All this makes clear that what we see on T.V., especially on the "news," is not an objective representation of reality, but a selection, according to a certain "standard" set by the program directors. While we assume that we are being presented with reality, we are being manipulated, and, after a while, we might adapt ourselves to the "standard" opinion. We receive our daily dose of brainwashing and manipulation, often without being aware of it. That is what we should realize more fully while we are watching the news, listening to the radio, or reading a newspaper. With a newspaper it is different, insofar as we realize newspaper editors are supposed to present the news in a slanted way. Our choice of newspaper gives us an opportunity to be selective, which we do not have in our system of news presentation via radio and T.V.

2. Opinion polls

Opinion polls are considered to be very important. Politicians as well as business people make extensive use of them. The production and marketing of a new product is always supported by marketing research, including extensive opinion polls. Advertising is often a matter of manipulating public opinion in the way the opinion polls have shown to be necessary, in order to make money with the new product.

Opinion polls are also used by politicians. The way they organize their election campaigns and the "promises" they make are based upon the results of such polls. Their whole presentation of political issues is supported by such research. Sometimes unpopular decisions are not made or are postponed because of an upcoming election. To know the public opinion is very important.

However, there is another effect. The result of such polls can be a self-fulfilling prophecy. If the public is presented every day with the results of opinion polls telling them, rightly or wrongly, that a certain party will achieve a landslide victory, it will undoubtedly have an enormous effect on the outcome of the election. The predicted landslide victory will come about, and the percentage of winning votes will be increased by the continuous prediction of this victory. Many people like to belong to the "winning" party. If they support the expected winner they can consider it their personal victory. "Their" man has won.

To a certain extent the same happens with public opinion when people hear the results of all kinds of "polls" and surveys. A poll seems to be an accurate presentation of public opinion with respect to a certain issue. It is a matter of statistics. Do statistics lie?

To say the least, we have to be careful to interpret statistics in the proper way, and to do so is a profession or a skill in its own right. It is important to consider the circumstances, the way the questions have been asked, and the selection of people who are questioned. There is always a certain percentage of people that do not answer. Is this group of "no opinion" equally spread over the whole group? That is certainly not always the case. The very nature of the issue can cause a particular group of people not to give their opinion on the questions, and in this way the outcome is a lopsided picture of reality.

Besides this effect, there is something else we have to be aware of. A question can be formulated in such a way that it includes a certain suggestion which leads the public in a certain direction. Take, for instance, the abortion issue. If a poll would be held asking people whether they are in favour of giving a pregnant girl the right to kill her baby before it is born if she does not want the baby, the majority might be opposed. However, if the wording of the question is whether a woman should have the right to decide what happens with her own body, the majority might be in favour. It depends, to a certain extent, on the way the question is formulated.

We can see the same with the peace movements. The majority of people are opposed to nuclear war. Of course! Who would be in favour! However, in many polls on actions and peace movements the impression is given that the question is whether you are in favour of or opposed to "peace," while the real question is whether such a peace can be achieved by a unilateral disarmament. To support or not support an action against the testing of cruise missiles is not a question of being in favour of or opposed to disarmament, but of whether or not such disarmament can be promoted by actions against, or even by doing away with, the whole development of these missiles. It is quite well possible that many "peace movements" do not serve the cause of peace and disarmament at all, but only encourage the Soviet Union to take a harder stand in the peace negotiations because the Western alliances are hampered anyway by these public demonstrations. The only result of this is a stepping up of the arms-race.

Let us be aware of the manipulation of public opinion. It takes place on a larger scale than most people believe. We will not escape this process, at least not as long as we do not fully realize what is going on.

3. Advertising

Did you ever think about the meaning of advertising? You can see all kinds of silly commercials on T.V. Do they make sense? Sometimes it seems that there is no message at all in the commercial. The content has little to do with the product that is advertised. You might wonder whether there is any customer who will buy the product because of such a commercial. An enormous amount of money is spent on these messages, however. It is big business. The advertisers are paying millions of dollars for it. They must have their reasons.

Market research proves the results. These companies are certainly not wasting their money on things which do not pay. How is that possible? The reason is that we are manipulated more than we are aware of. You might think that the contents of a commercial does not affect you, but the opposite is true.

Did you ever notice how often children are used in commercials? There are at least two reasons for that. In the first place the participation of children in such messages makes the whole matter more touching and affective for adults. That is one important reason.

There is another. Practice has proved that the influence of children upon the buying pattern of the parents is much greater than many of us realize. Market research shows that, through the continuous repetition of a message, some words or brand names are imprinted on the minds of children as well as adults. Through a seemingly meaningless commercial the brand name is associated with a nice experience, a happy feeling, or with desirable circumstances. The brand name becomes a word in its own right. Statistics have proved that sometimes a brand name is identified with a certain product in general.

Children take over this habit. When their parents go shopping with them, the children do not ask for a certain product but simply use a brand name which has been engraved on their minds. It even happens that the nice experience pictured in the commercial reminds them of the brand name. When something happens, they quote or whisper the name of the related product.

That is the psychological effect inherent in this system of advertising. You might think that it does not affect you, but the opposite is true. Their is a complete philosophy behind this advertising business. The large companies would not spend such enormous amounts of money on their commercials if practice had not proved that it is money well spent.

It is important that we realize these things. The people of the world have their tactics. Business people use this "manipulation" of public opinion. Politicians make it part and parcel of their campaigns. Also Satan is using his refined methods to lead people astray. I am afraid that we are not aware enough of these things, and the result is that we easily fall into a trap. Let us be alert! Being too naive can be dangerous. While I do not want to suggest that we use the same sophisticated psychological techniques in our education and in our evangelism, we can learn a lot from others when we notice what is going on — be it alone that we are on the alert. The continuous stream of advertising, of commercials during a newscast or even of ads in a newspaper, might have a greater impact on our life than we realize. What counts for commercials is even more applicable to modern entertainment and the watching of T.V. in general. It does not leave us untouched. There is an old Greek saying which goes: "Constant dropping wears away a stone." The same is true for people who receive their daily dose of indoctrination via the commercials. In the end it has its effect.

4. Brainwashing

Brainwashing means causing someone to change his mind by means which are not limited to reason or force. It is a form of systematic indoctrination by psychological manipulation, to undermine or change someone's opinion. Brainwashing plays a larger role in modern society, and also in our personal life, than most people realize. It might look silly to repeat the same message endlessly, but it is effective. The "action groups" and "movements" in our society have proved to be effective. No matter how unrealistic a message is, if you repeat it endlessly, eventually it will stick. These are the tactics of many "movements." We might consider some actions to be foolish, but let us not underestimate the tactics and the effects.

Nowadays we notice a selective indignation. People seem to be very upset about certain things, while other events hardly cause any reaction. Why is this?

There is certainly a philosophy behind it. More often than not it is a well-planned strategy. I already mentioned the peace movements and the actions against the testing of cruise missiles. The same can be said about the actions against the killing of wolves. Is that really such a big deal? Can the general public evaluate what the impact is on the survival of the one species at the cost of the other? Only a few are able to make a reasonable judgment. Still it is an issue that received extensive coverage in the news. The length of the news item about these things is not always in proportion to the importance of the issues. But many people get excited about it. "How do they dare to kill these 'innocent,' 'poor' wolves?" And yet, it is only a matter of a well-founded decision of the government with respect to wildlife.

I call this selective indignation, because people get excited simply because of the attention paid to it by the news media, while we do not notice much indignation or excitement about other developments which might be much more dangerous. In my book, *Like Living Stones*, I mentioned experiments, which are well underway, to fertilize human ova with the sperm of an animal and to fertilize animal eggs with human sperm. These laboratory experiments are a very dangerous threat to the human race. These fertilizations in vitro can lead, not only to a manipulation of public opinion, but to a manipulation of, and experiments with, human beings. However, little attention is paid to it. We hardly hear any reaction or criticism. Hardly any indignation is expressed via the news media. Why? Because it is not important? I consider these developments much more important than the killing of a certain number of wolves. Also in this way the public is manipulated and "brainwashed."

Fortunately there are many actions in our country against abortion and a relatively broad coverage is still given to these actions in the newscasts. Let us be thankful for this awareness of murder. Probably we, as Christians could do more to strengthen the cry against this threat to human life. The same counts for actions against euthanasia. Let us try, wherever we can, to stop or slow down the process of rejection of the divine ordinances for human life. It certainly does not depend on our effort, but the Lord has called us to be witnesses in this world. Let our voice be heard in a world in which the commandments of the Lord are considered to be of hardly any value.

5. Literature

What is happening to the habit of reading good books and magazines? Much time is spent, also in Christian families, watching T.V. Little time is spent on reading good books. It is important that we try to reverse this trend. More time should be spent on active education and active entertainment. Although watching T.V. has a greater impact on our children than we often are aware of, it is not an active education. It certainly teaches something, but not in the way we want. It manipulates our children and shapes their minds. Let us try to reverse this trend so that children learn to appreciate a good book. In that way they can study and become acquainted with all kinds of issues. They can form their own opinion and learn to resist the influence of the modern mass media. The necessity of reading more counts not only for children, but for all of us. The Bible study societies are important, but they are often not very much attended. We can only benefit from such societies if we personally put effort in it. Preparation for a meeting should not consist merely of reading a few things about the topic to be dealt with. No, we should put more effort into reading and studying in general. To read a good book or article in a magazine or newspaper can be a real help in shaping our opinion on certain issues. Let us not forget that the devil is at work. He is going around like a roaring wolf, seeking whom he can destroy. Be on your guard. In Hosea 4:6 the LORD warns us, "My people are destroyed for lack of knowledge." This might be one of our weakest points. T.V. and radio are a danger for family life. We can have extensive discussions about whether we should do away with it completely, or whether there are still certain programs we can watch. We can have lengthy discussions about the pros and the cons. But one of the most important aspects is that it makes people passive, opinionless, and thus an easy target for manipulation.

Are we too busy to read a book or an article? Do we have no time for it? Adding up the time spent watching T.V. and listening to the radio might give a different picture.

The Bible teaches us clearly that we must have our own life-style. Is that really the case? Do we dare to be different? Do we dare to show what it means to belong to Christ? In order to be able to survive in this world and to resist and overcome all the attacks of the power of darkness, we have to put on the whole armor of God as mentioned in Ephesians 6.

In the midst of a world full of indoctrination and manipulation we have to stand firm, equipped "with knowledge and all discernment, so that we may approve what is excellent, and may be pure and blameless for the day of Christ, filled with all the fruits of righteousness which come through Jesus Christ, to the glory and praise of God" (Philippians 1:9-11).

CHAPTER ELEVEN

The importance of prayer

1. Ora et labora

An old Latin proverb says: *Ora et labora.* That means: pray and work. This saying teaches us an important lesson. We have to adhere to it in all circumstances of life. It should be more than just another wise word. It has to become a living reality in our lives. To pray and to work should always go together. The one cannot go without the other. This saying points to a danger in two directions. The Word of God teaches us that it is in vain to work without prayer. Psalm 127:1 says: "Unless the LORD builds the house, those who build it labour in vain." But we also confess that, if we ignore our task and responsibility, if we do not work faithfully, our prayer is just some idle words. James 2:26 says: "Faith apart from works is dead."

In this chapter I will deal with both aspects of prayer.

2. Working without praying

It is in vain to work without praying. That is what the Bible clearly says in Psalm 127. After verse 1, quoted above, this psalm continues: "Unless the LORD watches over the city, the watchman stays awake in vain. It is in vain that you rise up early and go late to rest, eating the bread of anxious toil; for He gives to His beloved sleep."

If the Lord does not bestow His blessing on our work, all our effort is in vain. It might look as if we have "success" in our life or in our business. The results might be very impressive. But we know by experience that it can be gone all of a sudden. The recent depression has shown how vulnerable and feeble wealth and prosperity is. This is true for the short-term results of our labour, but even more so in the long run, especially when we think about the lasting or everlasting consequences. In Revelation 14:13 we read: "Blessed are the dead who die in the Lord henceforth. 'Blessed indeed,' says the Spirit, 'that they may rest from their labour, for their deeds follow them!' "

We all know this. At least we are supposed to. But do we live and act accordingly? I am afraid we do not. We all work hard. We are all very busy with our job, with our studies, with fixing our own house, our car or what have you. But do we really pray for all these things? Is it a living reality for us that without the blessing of the Lord our labour is in vain? Do we have our priorities straight?

We are involved in and busy with evangelism or home mission. We speak about people in other churches, and we are concerned about the developments in this world. We are frightened by the increasing lawlessness and by the spirit of revolution which is becoming evident everywhere. But do we also pray for those who are in danger of going astray and have been caught in the entangling net of the evil one?

In the Bible study societies we study the Word of God (that is, if we participate in these activities at all). We try to find the right attitude and approach to all kinds of practical matters. That is not always easy, for we sometimes have different opinions about certain matters. But do we really pray that the Lord may guide us by His Holy Spirit and show us the way we have to go?

We are confronted by the problems in social life. Unemployment, recession, and (in other parts of the world) famine and starvation. There is not much we can do. We talk about it and we are frightened by what we read, hear and see on the news. But do we really pray to the Lord to gant relief, and do we expect the help from Him alone?

Sometimes we feel powerless, unable to do anything. That can be very frustrating. In such a situation we quite often hear the remark: the only thing we can do is to pray. That might be true and it sounds very pious, but sometimes it is a sign of desperation, a last resort: let us try; while it may not help, it does not hurt either; we have nothing to lose; there is nothing else and nothing better we can do anyway. After we have tried everything, we finally take refuge to prayer. If that is our attitude, we are very late with our prayer. We apparently do not expect too much from it. We try to do it in our own strength rather than depend on the help of the Lord.

I am afraid that this is too often our attitude, although we are not always aware of it. However, in this way we underestimate the effect and the power of our prayers. The prayer of the children of the Lord can have world-shocking effects. In James 5:16 we read: "The prayer of a righteous man has great power in its effects." Do we really expect such great things as the result of our prayer? Or do we only use prayer as a last resort after everything else has failed? In James 5:17,18 we read: "Elijah was a man of like nature with ourselves and he prayed fervently that it might not rain, and for three years and six months it did not rain on the earth. Then he prayed again and the heaven gave rain, and the earth brought forth its fruit." That does not mean that we always receive an answer in the way Elijah did, but it certainly shows us that the LORD uses the prayer of believers and that He can and will do great things in answer to our prayers. However, He will do it according to His divine plan. We have to be patient. Sometimes when we pray and the Lord does not answer our prayers immediately or in the way we want it, we get upset — just like children who do not get their way. When we pray, we must trust that the Lord, as a Father, hears our prayers and that He will give us all we need according to His wisdom. We have to do our task, we have to work hard, we have to fulfil our mandate, and we have to live up to our own human responsibility, but we have to do it in the awareness that we have to work *and* to pray. Without the blessing of the Lord our effort is in vain.

3. Praying without working

In the previous section we saw that our work is in vain without prayer. Now we will pay attention to the other side of the matter. Our prayer becomes a matter of idle words if we do not work diligently and act responsibly. That is what the Heidelberg Catechism, for example, teaches us from the Word of God.

Our Lord Jesus Christ taught His disciples to pray. He taught them, and also us, to use the perfect prayer, as we can find in the Bible - not to use the Lord's Prayer always and only, but as an example to us how to pray, and to show us what belongs to a prayer that the Lord is pleased with and will hear. In Lord's Days 45 - 52 of the Heidelberg Catechism we can find the explanation of this prayer.

Lord's Day 48 speaks about the second petition: "Thy kingdom come." That is not some sort of a pious wish like: we hope so; we hope that Thy kingdom might come after all; we hope and pray, and now we will wait and see what happens. We should not pray without working. On the contrary. Read Answer 123 of the Heidelberg Catechism. Thy kingdom come means: "So rule us by Thy Word and Spirit that more and more we *submit* to Thee." The second petition puts us to work. We pray, but at the same time we have to work.

It is the same with the third petition "Thy will be done . . . ." That is not a wish: we hope and trust that Thy will will be done, and that Thy plan will be fulfilled. No, Answer 124 says: "Grant that we and all men may *deny* our own will, and without any murmuring *obey* Thy will, for it alone is good. Grant also that everyone may *carry out the duties* of his office and calling as willingly and faithfully as the angels in heaven." Also this petition puts us to work. We have to obey and to fulfil the will of God. The same is true for all six petitions. It is always: pray and work, *ora et labora*.

Is that a living reality in our life? Do we think when we pray? Prayer can become just another custom. We can fall into a rut. According to tradition, we open and close our meetings with prayer. Or, is it more than a tradition? If so, then we have to work hard and we have to exert ourselves to reach the goal. If we do not prepare for meetings by reading up on the topic, if we do not try to get involved in the discussion to find answers to the many questions and to understand the message, our prayer for a blessing upon our study meeting becomes idle words. Pray and work!

This applies to all situations in everyday life. In the sixth petition we pray: "Bring us not into temptation, but deliver us from the evil one." Answer 127 shows us the meaning of this petition: ". . . Strengthen us by the power of Thy Holy Spirit, so that . . . we . . . always firmly resist our enemies, until we finally obtain the complete victory." That is a clear instruction. We have to offer strong resistance! We are allowed to pray: "Bring us not into temptation," and we can trust in the Lord. He is always willing and able to help us in time of need. But we should not *seek* the temptation or put ourselves in a position in which we know that we will be exposed to strong temptations. That would not only reduce our prayer to idle words; it would contradict our prayer and make it a farce. Also in this respect praying and working have to go together.

4. What is prayer?

This question may seem redundant. Doesn't everyone know what prayer is?

I am not so sure. There are discussions these days about the meaning of prayer and the question whether it has a meaning at all. The opinions on the subject appear to be miles apart. For a lot of people prayer is something that belongs to the imaginary world of children and some antiquated and conservative older people. Prayer presupposes that there is someone to speak to, someone who is listening. Prayer is a thing of the past. It might still belong to the imaginary world of undeveloped people, but it has no place in the minds and lives of well-educated modern people. Prayer has been replaced by meditation and that is why especially the Eastern religions seem to be very attractive to modern man. People like devotion, meditation and religion, but they do not believe in a real God who dwells in heaven and listens to us. Even modern theologians reason along these lines. How is it possible for one divine being to listen to so many millions of people praying all at the same time? How can one God listen to all of them and answer their prayers?

I do not feel obliged to fight this heresy with extensive refutations. We simply believe and go by what Holy Scripture teaches us in many places; for instance, in James 5:16: "The prayer of a righteous man has great power in its effects," and in Matthew 7:11: "Your Father in heaven will give good things to those who ask Him!" We should never underestimate the effect and the power of our prayers.

About such prayers I will make some remarks in what follows. What are the requirements for such a prayer, and what should be the contents of it? What are we allowed to ask for, what are we even *required* to ask for, and what are we not allowed to ask for?

You may wonder whether it is right to deal with prayer in this way. Can we set standards and requirements? Is prayer not such an intimate matter that no one should interfere? Is it not something just between the Lord and the person who is praying? Is prayer not something that has to come right from the bottom of our hearts? Does a "discussion" of the requirements of prayer not make prayer less natural and spontaneous?

Such questions are often asked but they arise from a completely wrong idea of what prayer is all about. Working and praying are two things which belong together. Would it be possible to judge someone's work and not his prayer? The Bible teaches us clearly that there are requirements for our work as well as for our prayer. We can even put it this way: praying is also working. Prayer is part of our "good works." Now this statement needs some explanation!

The expression that our prayers are part of our good works seems to go in the wrong direction. However, that is certainly not the case. It is a conclusion of what the Heidelberg Catechism teaches us. Let us have

a closer look at what our confession says in this respect.

In Lord's Day 32 we confess that "we have been delivered from our misery by grace alone through Christ, without any merit of our own." Therefore the question is asked: "Why must we yet do good works?" The answer is clear. "That with our whole life we may show ourselves thankful to God for His benefits, and that He may be praised by us." Good works are a matter of thankfulness. We do not do good works to deserve something. Christ has paid for our sins. He has made full satisfaction. We are saved by mere grace, without any merit of ours. But through His Holy Spirit Christ renews us after His own image, that we should show ourselves thankful to God for His benefits. Our good works are the result of His work in our lives and the fruits of the work of the Holy Spirit in our hearts. It is our thankfulness to the Lord.

What are the "good works" which we are supposed to do? Answer 91 of the Heidelberg Catechism says: "Only those which are done out of true faith, in accordance with the law of God, and to His glory."

Doing good works is a matter of thankfulness, and the most important part of it is prayer! That is what Answer 116 says. Prayer is not just *a part* of the good works done in thankfulness to the Lord; it is *the most important part* of our thankfulness. And the Lord *requires* from us such a prayer.

This shows us that prayer is not just an intimate relationship between the Lord and the believer, and not something that has to come spontaneously from the bottom of the heart, without applying any rules. No, it is a requirement, and there are rules and regulations. Of course, it does have to come spontaneously from the bottom of our hearts, otherwise it would be hypocrisy. But that is not *enough*. It also must be governed by the Law of the Lord and be in accordance with Biblical guidelines. Because prayer is part of the good works the Lord requires of us, it has to meet strict standards. Just because we do not deserve anything by it, does not make it any less necessary.

In this way we are going to deal with prayer. We are going to listen to what the Word of God says about it and what we confess in the Heidelberg Catechism. Successively, we will pay attention to different aspects of prayer.

5. Childlike prayer

How do we pray? That is an important question. Sometimes our prayer seems to be a sort of inventory or checklist of all our wishes, desires, and complaints. We bring it all before the Lord so that He can fulfil all our wishes. And when the Lord does not act immediately according to our requests, we get upset and impatient.

But that is not the right attitude. That is not the way our Lord Jesus Christ has taught us to pray. The first and most important thing in our prayer should not be the fulfilment of all *our* desires, but the glory and honour of the Lord. The main issue has to be: His Name, His Kingdom and His Will.

Prayer is a service of gratitude. A real prayer can be said only by a true believer, by someone who knows that Jesus Christ is his Saviour and that God is his Father. That is what we learn from Christ's teaching. Prayer is something that has to be learned. It does not just come, spontaneously, from the bottom of our hearts as a natural reaction. It has to be a matter of submission and obedience to the Lord. Of course, it also has to come from the bottom of our hearts, otherwise it would be hypocritical. But it has to be more than that. Lord's Day 45 mentions the requirements for a prayer God is pleased with and will hear. The apostle Paul says in Romans 8:26, "We do not know how to pray as we ought, but the Spirit himself intercedes for us with sighs too deep for words."

In Matthew 7 our Lord Jesus Christ teaches us to pray like children, with childlike trust in God our Father. To pray like children is not easy. It is something we have to learn; we have to train ourselves. In Matthew 7:9 and 11 Jesus says: "What man of you, if his son asks him for bread, will give him a stone? . . . If you then, who are evil, know how to give good gifts to your children, how much more will your Father who is in heaven give good things to those who ask Him!"

The meaning of this example is probably not clear to everyone. Who would give a child a stone instead of bread? The child would not even accept the stone but would throw it away. This example does not seem to fit, does it? However, we have to consider the situation in Jesus time. His audience understood the meaning better than we do. In that time people did not have sliced white bread like we have nowadays. They did not use yeast or baking pans. They used sour dough and baked the bread in an oven which was heated by a wood fire, or they baked the bread over an open fire. Their bread was more or less shaped like our buns, but was flatter. Their bread was not as airy and light as ours, but was rather heavy. The stones, referred to, were not building bricks as we know them, but pieces of pumice stone, as could be found on the shores of the Jordan River and in the hill country. These stones had about the same shape, colour and weight as their bread.

When we consider this, we understand what it means to give a child a stone instead of bread. It would be a dirty trick, because the child, trusting his parents, would accept the stone, probably not noticing the difference, and put the stone in his mouth only to break his teeth and discover that it was not bread at all.

Well, our Lord Jesus Christ asks, "What father would deal with his child in such a way?" No real father, who cares for his children, would do so. Much less our heavenly Father. He never deceives us when He gives us something. He never fools us by giving us something that later turns out to be dangerous or the opposite of what we thought it was. That is the meaning of the example of the bread and the stone.

But there is also another message in it as well. It teaches us to pray like children, who trust their parents.

Parents would never give their children a stone instead of bread, but sometimes they do let their children wait. If a child comes home from school and asks for a slice of bread, his mother might say: "No, that would spoil your appetite for supper. Go outside and play for a while. I will call you when it is suppertime." Or if the child asks for a candy, his mother might say: "No. Here is an apple. That is better for you." Parents know what is good for their children. They will give their children all they need, but children have to learn that what their parents give them is not always what they asked for. It might be something that is even better for them than what they asked for.

It is the same with our prayers and the way our Father in heaven deals with us. He always listens to us and provides us with everything we need. But He might give us something else than we asked for, or let us wait until it is His time. He knows what we need much better than we do.

If we put it this way, the question may arise: Why then pray at all? If our Father knows what we need anyway, even better than we do, and if He gives, not what *we* think is good for us, but what is good according to His divine wisdom, why do we bother to pray? Let's just leave it up to Him to provide us with all we need. It's no use to pray.

The answer to this question is given in Lord's Day 45. "God will give His grace and the Holy Spirit only to those who constantly and with heartfelt longing ask Him for these gifts and thank Him for them." Is that not the way parents deal with their children? They have to learn to ask politely. They should not rush into the house and grab a cookie or a candy. If they want something, they should first ask Dad or Mom. Why? To show their respect and to recognize the authority of their parents. They also have to learn to say: Thank you. They should realize that it is the parents who provide them with all they need. They must be thankful and show their gratitude.

The same is true for our relationship with the Lord, our Father in heaven. He knows what we need. He is willing and able to give us everything, according to His wisdom, but He wants us to ask for it. In our prayer we have to show our respect, our trust in Him, and our thankfulness for all He gives us every day. That is what Answer 120 calls "the childlike reverence and trust toward God which should be basic to our prayer."

6. Unanswered prayers

Is there such a thing as unanswered prayer? It all depends on what we mean by it. In Isaiah 65:24 we read: "Before they call I will answer, while they are yet speaking I will hear." But we do not see it happen. Isaiah is speaking there (according to verse 17) about "new heavens and a new earth." In our present situation the opposite seems to be true. We call but we do not receive any answer. We speak but it seems that no one hears. We pray, sometimes for many years, but nothing happens. And yet our Lord Jesus Christ says in Matthew 7:7 and 8: "Ask and it will be given to you . . . For everyone who asks receives." How can we tally these two with each other? Is there such a thing as unanswered prayers or not?

The answer to this question can be found in Matthew 7:7-12. Our heavenly Father listens to His children. He never gives us a stone instead of bread. He never fools us, but He answers our prayers as a real Father.

That means that He sometimes let us wait, perhaps way too long in our opinion, or that He gives us something else than we have asked for. Let us, His children, trust in Him and His care. Let us not, like impatient children, get upset and complain that the Lord does not *answer*. That happens quite often. But that is not because there are unanswered prayers; that is our shortsightedness. We as children do not *see* the hand of our Father. But He is at work nevertheless.

It is not always easy to accept this - especially not when we are really in trouble and have to wait a very long time. Sometimes our faith is put to the test. We have to learn to accept the will of our Father. We must trust in Him and believe that He knows and gives us what is good for us.

7. The contents of our prayer

What belongs to a faithful prayer? What are we allowed to ask for, and what not? Are we allowed to ask for anything we wish? Yes, we are, at least if we do it with childlike reverence toward and trust in God. That means that we must be aware of the fact that our Father knows what is good for us.

There are even things we *have to* ask for. Question 117 of the Heidelberg Catechism asks: "What belongs to such a prayer which pleases God and is heard by Him?" The answer is that we have to call upon Him "for all that He has *commanded* us to pray." That means that there are things we *have to* ask for. It shows us clearly that there are requirements for our prayer. It is not just a matter of our personal feelings and emotions; it is a *commandment* of the Lord.

In the next Lord's Day the Heidelberg Catechism shows us what the contents of our prayer should be. Of foremost importance is the honour and glory of the Lord, His Name, His Kingdom and His Will.

We pray: Thy Kingdom come. That is not a wish. At the end of the Lord's Prayer it says: For thine *is* the Kingdom. We pray for the coming of the Kingdom of heaven and at the same time we confess: Thine *is* the Kingdom. We know that His Kingdom is already at hand and is already coming. In Answer 128 we confess: "As our King, having power over all things, Thou art both willing and able to give us all that is good."

We are allowed to ask for anything, as long as we do it with the confession: not my will but Thy will be done. We do not have the promise that the Lord will give us everything we ask for. There are certain things which He has promised us. There are things we can ask without saying: "If it pleases Thee," because we know that the Lord is pleased to give it. We are allowed to plead on His promises, to use our baptism, to ask for the forgiveness of our sins and the guidance of the Holy Spirit "for Christ's sake." That means: we know that the Lord will give us what we are asking, because He has given us His promise. We can count on it. We do not have to add, "If it pleases Thee" or "Thy will be done," because we know the will of the Lord in this repect; we know that He is pleased to hear us.

There are also things the Lord has not promised to give us. But we are allowed to ask for these things if we add: "Not as I will but as Thou wilt."

Some people wonder whether we are allowed to ask for the impossible. Are we allowed to ask for restoration to health when we know that someone is incurably ill? Are we allowed to ask for recovery when we know that it is impossible? Are we allowed to ask for a miracle?

Yes, we are. For what is a "miracle?" What is impossible? When is someone "incurably ill?" There are miracles in our life, at least if we are willing to see them! Every birth is a miracle. And in the sight of the Lord no one is "incurably" ill. We are always allowed to ask for recovery, although we do not always receive what we ask for. Sometimes the will of the Lord is different. But because we do not know the will of the Lord in this respect, we are allowed to pray. As long as we do it with reverance and not as impatient children who want to have their way, and who get upset if they do not succeed. We should never oppose the will of the Lord. We always have to submit to Him and His decisions.

Another question is whether someone who is sick always *has to* ask for recovery. That is certainly not the case. We very often see that the Lord "prepares" someone for the end. First we hear a fervent prayer for recovery. After a while the contents of the prayer changes. More emphasis is put on receiving the strength to carry on and to accept the suffering. I have often seen on visits and in discussions with terminally ill people that they grow in a certain direction, until, finally, they pray that the Lord will take them away and relieve them from their suffering. They look forward to the end, to be united with Christ. We are allowed to pray for the end. We do not know what the will of the Lord is. Therefore we say: "Not as I will, but as Thou wilt." And if the Lord does not give us what we ask for, we have to accept His decision as the right one.

It also happens that people who are prepared to die and who ask the Lord to take them away, recover. They may find it very difficult to go back to normal life. They wish they could have died. That happens, and we can understand how people feel in such a situation.

What we have to learn, in all circumstances of life, is to accept the will of our heavenly Father. He gives us all we need, every time we ask Him. He gives us strength to carry the burden we have to bear. He gives us the strength when we *need* it. He does not give us the strength to die as long as we have the task to live. We have no promise that He will give us today what we need tomorrow or next year. According to Hebrews 4:16 we have a High Priest in heaven from whom we will receive mercy and grace to help in time of need. Just in time. Not earlier, but also never too late.

8. The power of prayer

We should never underestimate the power of our prayers. I already mentioned James 5:16. There we read: "The prayer of a righteous man has great power in its effects." The meaning of this text has to be understood from what follows in the verses 17 and 18. There the apostle uses the example of the prophet Elijah. "Elijah was a man of like nature with ourselves and he prayed fervently that it might not rain, and for three years and six months it did not rain on the earth. Then he prayed again and the heaven gave rain, and the earth brought forth its fruit."

This shows us the power of prayer. It can move heaven and earth. Does that mean that we, by our prayers, can rule and command everything? Can we simply command the heavens to give rain and they will obey? In Matthew 17:20 Jesus says: "For truly, I say to you, if you have faith as a grain of mustard seed, you will say to this mountain, 'Move from here to there,' and it will move; and nothing will be impossible to you." Does that mean that we have such a power at our disposal at any time, to use it the way we wish? No, certainly not! That is what the preachers of so-called faith healing try to make us believe. If you pray, or rather, if they pray for and with you, you will be healed at any time, no matter what your disease might be. Is that true? Do they rightly refer to James 5 and Matthew 17 in this respect?

There has been much discussion on this issue. The question is not whether there is such a thing as "faith healing" or whether health can be restored as a result of prayer. The question is whether we *see* the relationship between our prayer and our recovery. Every day people are healed as a result of their prayers. When a Christian receives recovery of health, we may see it as the work of the Lord and as an answer to prayers. While the Lord uses the means: medications prescribed by a doctor, surgery, or some other type of hospital treatment, it is still the Lord who works, and it is a result of our prayers. The prayer of a righteous man has great power in its effects.

We must pray in a childlike manner, however, believing and confessing that our heavenly Father knows what is good for us and that He will give us all we need. The big demonstrations of so-called faith healers are often mere manifestations of their own human pretences. People try to make us believe that they can work miracles and that they have at their disposal the power to make decisions the Father has reserved for Himself. It is an activity to the glory of the "faith healers" rather than to the glory of God.

And it certainly does not really help the sick. Many sick people, who in true faith could carry the burden of their illness, have gone to such faith healers without receiving recovery. Afterwards they had great difficulty accepting their situation, because the faith healer led them to believe that it was because of a lack of faith on their part that they did not receive recovery. Some believers have almost lost their faith on account of it.

We always have to pray with childlike trust in the Lord. We do not have any promises that the Lord will give recovery to all who pray for it. While Jesus was on earth He healed many who were sick, but not all of them. Concerning the man who was born blind Jesus said in John 9:3: "It was not that this man sinned, or his parents, but that the works of God might be manifest in him." Job lost all his possessions, not because of a lack of faith, but to show the victory of God's grace in his life, in spite of the temptation of the devil. We do not always understand why the Lord deals with us as He does, but we have to trust, like children trust their parents, that He knows what is best for us. And yet we are allowed to

116

pray, continually, even when everything seems to be against us.

Sometimes we hear people say: the only thing we can do is pray. That can be a dangerous attitude. The *only* thing we can do? That sounds like a last resort: when everything else fails, we have to rely on prayer. But that should not be our attitude. We should always *begin* with prayer. Without the blessing of the Lord all our effort is in vain. Pray and work. Without prayer our work does not help. We have to confess that prayer is not just a last resort. Our attitude should not be: while it may not help, it does not hurt either. No, prayer is the most powerful weapon we have — at least if we pray in childlike faith, both for ourselves and for each other. That brings us to our next point.

9. Praying for others

In our conversations we talk about others. We are concerned that others might go astray. We *talk* about others, but do we also pray for them? We are concerned about the increasing lawlessness in the world and about the spirit of revolution which is becoming evident everywhere. We are concerned about the hunger and misery in Third World countries and about the persecution of Christians in many parts of the world. We feel powerless and think that we cannot do much about it! But do we really bring all these matters before the countenance of the Lord in our prayer? Do we realize the power of our prayers? Evangelism might be important, but it is not the first and most important thing. First we must pray for others, also for repentance and conversion of those who are going astray.

Our Lord Jesus Christ has taught us to pray: "Forgive *us our* debts." Not: "Forgive *me my* debts" — singular — but "forgive *us our* debts" — plural. That is not an attitude of "safety in numbers." It is not a matter of "hiding among the crowd." The statement: "We are all sinners; nobody is perfect," is an easy and cheap attempt to escape our responsibilities. It is an attempt to avoid a personal confession of sins.

That should not be our attitude. We have to confess our sins. We have to be very specific before the Lord when we ask forgiveness of our sins. But at the same time we have to pray for the salvation of others, for the forgiveness of their sins.

In the fifth petition our Lord Jesus Christ taught us to pray: "Forgive us our debts, as we also have forgiven our debtors." To forgive our neighbours is not just a condition for receiving forgiveness of our sins. It is more than that. The Heidelberg Catechism calls it "the evidence of Thy grace in us that we are fully determined whole heartedly to forgive our neighbour." That is a strong and clear statement. If we are not prepared to forgive our neighbour, then we do not have the "evidence of God's grace in us." Then we must consider whether our sins are forgiven. A good tree bears fruit.

This shows us that prayer is not a strictly personal thing. It is a matter of the communion of saints. This communion has to be shown in the way we care for each other and in the way we pray for others.

Our prayer should also have a personal aspect, especially when we confess our sins before the Lord.

10. Prayer as personal confession of sins

The Reformed churches do not practice penance or the confession of sins before a priest or other "clergyman," as they do in the Roman Catholic Church. We do not confess our secret sins before men in order to receive forgiveness of sins. But we do need to make a personal confession of sins — not before man, but before the Lord. That is not always possible during a family prayer before or after meals. There are many things in life which are not known to others. Therefore, besides family prayers, we all need personal prayers, to bring before the Lord everything that bothers us, especially our personal sins and shortcomings.

When we confess our sins before the Lord we should be specific. It is not enough to say: "Forgive us our sins." If the Lord would answer and ask: "Which sin do you mean," I am afraid that many of us would hesitate and say: "I do not know, I am not aware of any sin." If that is the case our prayers become idle words. Let us mention our sins before the Lord. Let us think about our shortcomings and ask forgiveness for specific transgressions of His commandments.

If we are not aware of our sins, there is something very basic missing in our life. The Heidelberg Catechism teaches us clearly in Lord's Day 1 that we first have to know how great our sins and misery are, and that only in this way we will be delivered from our sins and misery and show our thankfulness to God for such deliverance. Without knowledge of our sins and misery we cannot live and die happily in the only comfort.

It is very unfortunate that there is sometimes a standstill in our prayers and, consequently, a decline in our spiritual life and in our relationship with the Lord. The reason is often a lack of awareness of our sins, and therefore also a lack of thankfulness to the Lord for the salvation in Jesus Christ. If that happens, we might even stop praying for a while.

11. When prayer is neglected

In the Canons of Dort (v,4) we read that the believers must constantly watch and pray because, "when they do not watch and pray, they not only can be drawn away . . . into serious and atrocious sins but . . . are sometimes actually drawn away."

Why do people stop praying? When we talk with people we hear all kinds of reasons. In what follows I will deal with a number of them.

Some ask: "Why should I pray? The Lord knows everything. He knows even better than I do and before I ask Him. He will give me what I need anyway. And if I ask for something which is not good for me, He will not give it; He will give me something else. Why should I bother the Lord with my wishes, if He has made His decision already long ago?"

Of course, we do not pray to the Lord to tell Him something new. That is correct. But the Lord has revealed Himself as our Father and He wants to be honoured as a Father in that we, in childlike reverence, go to Him with everything that is in our hearts. We have to show that we expect everything out of His hand and must ask Him just as a child asks his parents.

If we stop praying, we lose the covenantal relationship and communication with our Father in heaven.

Others ask: "Why should I pray? It does not change anything. The Lord has already decided everything. We have to take things as they come anyway."

Also this seemingly logical reasoning does not hold water. Of course, we believe that the Lord, in His providence, rules the whole world and knows everything that will happen. But *we* do not know the "secret counsel" of the Lord. We have our own task and responsibility, and our prayer also has a place in God's providence and in His eternal counsel. When we are sick, we do not know whether the Lord will give us restoration of health nor when or how the Lord will accomplish it. We do go to the doctor and use the medication he prescribes. Also the use of medicines is part of God's providence. The same is true for our prayers. The Lord will use our prayers to give recovery. The prayer of a righteous man has great power in its effects.

Still others say: "The Lord is so far away. I cannot pray anymore. It seems that He does not hear and does not answer. It seems that God does not exist. I have lost everything. I am uncertain about everything. It scares me, but I cannot change the situation. I just have to live with it."

This happens among believers more often than we are aware of. It does not always come into the open, but many church members go through a crisis like this at one time or another. That is why we should talk about these things with one another, to support each other as members of the one body of Christ. There are all sorts of causes of this feeling of being lost. But one thing is clear: it is always an attack of the devil. He tries to lead us astray.

Sometimes people have to fight against a certain sin in their life and they fall back into this sin time and again, until they surrender completely. However, in such a situation we should take to heart what we confess in Lord's Day 52: "Wilt Thou, therefore, uphold and strengthen us by the power of Thy Holy Spirit, so that in this spiritual war we may not go down to defeat, but always firmly resist our enemies, until we finally obtain the complete victory." We can count on the promises of the Lord. When we fall into Satan's strainer, Christ will not forsake us. In Luke 22:31 He gave us the promise that He will pray for us that our faith may not fail. We should not despair of God's mercy. Even when we cannot find the words to pray, the Spirit himself prays for us with sighs too deep for words (Romans 8:26). In such a situation we have to fight with everything that is in us. That is why we need, even more than in other situations, to be strengthened by prayer. We are allowed to call on the Name of the Lord and to hold onto His promises.

It is also possible that people stop praying because of indifference, because there is no fight at all and no awareness of sins. In discussions with such people we notice that they are not really distressed by their sins. They think they are doing very well. They are satisfied with themselves. In such a situation we cannot expect a real prayer. If people do not see their sins, why should they seek salvation and redemption? And what do they have to be thankful for?

Our personal prayer should never become just another habit; it should always be a living reality. Besides our personal prayer, we should also have our common prayers, our joint prayer, together with others within the communion of saints. This is our next point.

12. Joint prayer

It is very important that we join in prayer as a family before and after meals. In some families it is the custom to be "silent" for a while. Everyone prays for himself and no one "leads" in prayer. Some parents seem to be hesitant to "speak up." It is a family devotions time without words.However, this is not good for more than one reason. In the first place it is difficult to concentrate on our prayer, when we know that others are waiting. If there is something special to be mentioned in prayer, we do not have the proper, restful atmosphere in such a situation to bring it before the Lord. Besides, it is important that children learn to pray at home. Once I heard of a child in kindergarten whose parents had a "silent" prayer at home before and after meals. The child apparently did not know what prayer really meant, for when he came home after the first day in kindergarten, he told his parents: "The teacher at school talks during prayer." The child did not understand that prayer means: speaking to the Lord. He knew only about closing his eyes, folding his hands and being silent for a little while. That shows us how important it is *that*, and *how*, we pray together in the family. It is basic instruction for the children.

Another aspect of our joint prayer is the communion of saints. We all are one in the Lord, and together we bring before His countenance all our needs. We pray for each other and we give thanks to the Lord for all His blessings. Such a joint prayer can be of great comfort and a source of strength for the whole family. When children have learned to pray together at home, they will also do it when they grow up.

Young people who are dating or are engaged try to get acquainted with each other in every respect. They have to share pleasures and disappointments, joy and sorrow. Together they learn to overcome the problems in their life and to fight against temptations. There will be tensions once in a while, especially when they are engaged for a long time. They have to protect each other and not take before marriage what is reserved for marriage only. Their greatest source of strength is joint prayer. But how often *do* they pray together?

Nowadays young people are very familiar with each other. There seem to be no secrets at all. But an important thing is missing, and that is joint prayer. One of the most important factors in getting to know the other person and in preparing for marriage is their spiritual unity. If the young people do not feel free to pray together while they are engaged, there is something wrong. Parents have to make their children familiar with joint prayer. If they have learned it at home, they will also practice it in their own life. Proverbs 22:6 says: "Train up a child in the way he should go, and when he is old he will not depart from it."

There are all kinds of situations in daily life when we can join in prayer. When we have company we discuss together all kinds of issues. There might be joy or concern. If we have discussed a sad situation, should we conclude: here is nothing we can do about it? Would it be much more comforting to pray together about it?

Unfortunately, that is not one of our strong points. We leave it up to the office-bearers to lead in prayer during an official visit. We pray at the beginning and at the end of our meals, and at the opening and closing of our meetings, but not when we have company. In this respect we can learn from others.

Of course, we have to be careful that such prayers do not become a meaningless routine. We have to pray with due respect to the Lord, confessing that He is our Father who knows what is good for us. So called "prayer sessions" can become a sort of superstitious way to "force" the Lord to do something. But *we* are in danger of underestimating the meaning and the importance of joint prayer.

13. Leading in prayer

I already mentioned that in some families no one leads in prayer. While there is "silence" for a moment, everyone is supposed to pray for himself. The reason for this is that no one feels free to lead in prayer.

I admit that leading in prayer is not an easy task. Especially when it has to be done on a regular basis, we have to be careful that it does not become a meaningless routine. We always have to realize to whom we are speaking. A minister, an elder, a teacher, or everyone who has to lead in prayer many times a day knows how great the danger is that it becomes a "routine." When we pray we have to do it with our whole heart. I can imagine that some have problems finding the right words when they have to lead in prayer. However, it is not important that we use nice, perfect phrases, but that we pray with our whole heart. The best place to learn this is at home, in the family.

The Pharisees had other practises. They used to pray on street corners and in marketplaces to be seen and heard by man. But Jesus condemned their practises. The tax collector, who beat his breast, saying, "God, be merciful to me, a sinner" went down to his home justified, rather than the Pharisee with his eloquent prayer.

14. Prayer training

Can we train our children to pray? How can we help someone who, for one reason or another, does not dare to lead in prayer? At Young People's Society meetings, and even Men's or Women's Society meetings, there are always some members who hesitate or refuse to lead in prayer when they are asked. Sometimes they even refuse to join a society, just to avoid the embarrassment.

The same happens in some families, where the parents do not lead in prayer. How do we help them? Can we "teach" someone to pray?

We certainly can! In Luke 11:2 we read that the disciples came to Jesus and asked Him: "Lord, teach us to pray, as John taught his disciples." The instruction, given by our Lord Jesus Christ on that occasion is important also for us today. Jesus taught His disciples to use the perfect prayer, called "The Lord's Prayer." Not that we should only and always use these words. No, it is given to us as a perfect example of how we are supposed to pray. Of course, we should also use our own words and bring before the Lord all our specific needs. But when someone has to lead in prayer, for instance, at the end of a meeting, and he is afraid that he cannot find the proper words, there is nothing wrong with using the Lord's Prayer. Nor is there something wrong with being prepared and having a prayer on paper. Let us never laugh at someone who stumbles or gets stuck and cannot find the right words.

In some families the parents ask their children to lead in prayer after meals. They take turns. The little ones have their own short prayer, and the older ones lead in prayer for the whole family. This is an excellent way to teach children to pray. They get used to it and feel their responsibility. It also makes them listen more carefully and attentively while others are leading in prayer. It is an important element of the training in their spiritual life. It also gives them the experience they need if they have to lead in prayer at a meeting or later in their own family. Prayer becomes a natural thing, as it is supposed to be.

Our prayers are sacrifices of thanksgiving. For a sacrifice we have to set high standards. At the same time, it has to come from the heart and it has to be in obedience to the Word of God. The Lord has taught us clearly that "to obey is better than sacrifice, and to hearken than the fat of rams" (I Sam. 15:22).

15. Joint prayer with unbelievers

Is it possible to pray with people who do not believe? This question can arise in a variety of situations. A nurse may be asked to lead in prayer in a child care center; a visitor in a hospital may be asked to pray with a group of people whom he does not even know. In some hospitals ministers are expected to pray with all the people in the room when he visits one of them.

This is a very delicate issue. We should try not to hurt the feelings of others, but we should be honest and obedient to the Lord in the first place. We have to consider the circumstances. Leading in prayer is always a difficult and delicate matter, but even more so when there are persons present who do not believe or who have completely different ideas about the service of the Lord. Still it is possible to lead in prayer in such situations, at least if we have sufficiently analyzed the circumstances. When a minister visits someone in a hospital and is asked to pray with all the people on the ward, he can do so.

However, there are two things we have to be aware of. In the first place a prayer should not be used to communicate with the listeners, but to speak to the Lord. We should not use prayer to bring the message of the gospel. That would be an abuse of prayer. Nor should we admonish the listeners via our prayer.

In the second place we have to realize that such a prayer is of a different nature than our joint prayers at home. If people have no objection to being present during our prayer, or if they ask us to lead in prayer, we can pray for others, even if they do not feel the same way we do. Such a prayer is not a matter of "communion of saints." But we may pray for the recovery of others; we may even pray that they find strength and comfort in the Lord. We may pray that the Holy Spirit work in their hearts. In this way we can pray with, or rather *for* unbelievers, if they want to be present during our prayer. We should never purposely or unnecessarily hurt the feelings of others by such a prayer. Our prayer should not become an indirect form of preaching or admonition. If we use such a prayer in the right way, it can be of great comfort to the listeners and it can give them food for thought. Before or after such a prayer we might have the opportunity to speak a few words about the gospel of salvation. Especially in a hospital situation many people are very receptive to such a message.

However, we should never compromise on the requirements set by the Word of God with respect to prayer. In each and every situation we have to remember that prayer is "the most important part of the thankfulness which God requires of us, and that God will give His grace and Holy Spirit only to those who constantly and with heartfelt longing ask Him for these gifts and thank Him for them" (Answer 116 of the Heidelberg Catechism).

In Question 117 of the Heidelberg Catechism we read: "What belongs to a prayer which pleases God and is heard by Him?" The answer is: "First, we must from the heart call upon the one true God only, who has revealed Himself in His Word, for all He has commanded us to pray. Second, we must thoroughly know our need and misery, so that we may humble ourselves before God. Third, we must rest on this firm foundation that, although we do not deserve it, God will certainly hear our prayer for the sake of Christ our Lord, as He has promised us in His Word."

". . . as He has promised us in His Word . . . ." Let us plead on these promises. Then we never pray in vain. And let us in the meantime do what we can and must do according to the Word of God.

Pray and work. *Ora et labora.*